UNCLE JOHN'S
Creature Feature

BATHROOM READER® FOR KIDS ONLY

UNCLE JOHN'S
Creature Feature

BATHROOM READER®
FOR KIDS ONLY

by the
Bathroom Readers'
Institute

Bathroom Readers' Press
Ashland, Oregon

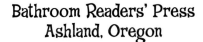

UNCLE JOHN'S
CREATURE FEATURE
BATHROOM READER®
FOR KIDS ONLY

Articles in this edition have been included from the following books:
Uncle John's Wild & Woolly Bathroom Reader for Kids Only © 2005,
Uncle John's Strange & Scary Bathroom Reader for Kids Only © 2006, and
Uncle John's Under the Slimy Sea Bathroom Reader for Kids Only © 2007.

For information, write:
Bathroom Readers' Institute
P.O. Box 1117, Ashland, OR 97520
www.bathroomreader.com

Cover design by Michael Brunsfeld

Illustrations by John Gaffey and Scott G. Brooks

ISBN-13: 978-1-60710-099-7 / ISBN-10: 1-60710-099-1

Library of Congress Cataloging-in-Publication Data

Uncle John's creature feature bathroom reader for kids only /
[the Bathroom Readers' Institute].
    p. cm.
ISBN 978-1-60710-099-7 (pbk.)
1. Wit and humor, Juvenile. 2. Animals—Humor.
3. Animals—Juvenile literature. 4. Curiosities and wonders—
Juvenile literature. I. Bathroom Readers' Institute (Ashland, Or.)
PN6166.U527 2010
081.02'07—dc22
                                        2009039315

Printed in Crawfordsville, Indiana, United States of America

Second printing: April 2010

2 3 4 5 6   14 13 12 11 10

READERS' RAVES

From some of our favorite readers!

"OK, I'll start by saying that *Uncle John's Bathroom Readers* are probably the greatest idea since PB & J! My entire family reads your books. We share, we trade, then we have little sit-downs about the funniest article of the day."

—**Brad**

"I'm 13 years old, and I'm a really big fan of your books. They rock!!!"

—**Rachel**

"I recently led my middle school team to second place in the 'Optimist Brain Bowl.' After every match, judges, teachers, and parents of the opposing team would come up to me, wondering how I knew so much. I simply smiled and said, 'I'd like to thank Uncle John and the entire BRI staff.'"

—**Jamie**

"If I had to choose between *Bathroom Readers* or home-work, *Bathroom Readers* would be what I would choose."

—**Wesley**

"I love your books!!!! I can never go to the bathroom without my mom yelling at me because I take soooo long reading my *Bathroom Readers*!"

—**Michael**

"I am a 6th grader, and I read my *Bathroom Readers* everywhere in the house at all times of day. I LOVE them!!!"
—**Jake**

"Your books are tremendous!!!! Stupendous!!!!! They're absolutely outstanding!!!!"
—**Angela**

"I just wanted to say how much I enjoy reading your books. They are really fun to read. I learn so much from them. Thank you."
—**Kathleen**

"I got one of your books for my birthday and I can't get off it. My parents think I'm too nerdy for my own good, but I think your books are better than words can say!"
—**Freeman**

"Your books are the best ever. EVER! My whole family loves them (even my little sister). You should do more stuff about ghosts because ghosts scare my sister."
—**Marvin**

"I love your *Bathroom Readers*. My grandma introduced them to me. Thank you, grandma! Keep those books coming, Uncle John!"
—**Jen**

TABLE OF CONTENTS

WILD & WOOLY

UNDER THE SLIMY SEA

STRANGE & SCARY

THANK YOU

The Bathroom Readers' Institute thanks those people whose help has made this book possible.

Gordon Javna	John Dollison
Jahnna Beecham	Melinda Allman
Malcolm Hillgartner	Christine DeGueron
Amy Miller	Lisa Meyers
John Gaffey	Amy Ly
Scott Brooks	Monica Maestas
Michael Brunsfeld	Sydney Stanley
Dale Champlin	JoAnn Padgett
Maggie McLaughlin	Dash and Skye
Jay Newman	Scarab Media
Brian Boone	Tom Mustard
Thom Little	Shobha Grace
Julia Papps	Porter the Wonder Dog
Jeff Altemus	Thomas Crapper

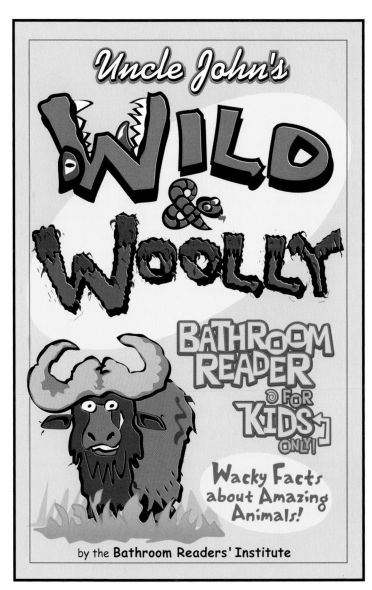

Uncle John's WILD & WOOLLY

BATHROOM READER FOR KIDS ONLY!

Wacky Facts about Amazing Animals!

by the **Bathroom Readers' Institute**

Intro-DOG-tion

H iya, Kids! Porter the Wonder Dog here. Uncle John asked me—his faithful pal—to write this introduction. What an honor! It's almost as fun as chasing my own tail! (But not quite.)

I think you're going to love this book. Why? Because it's not *a* book— it's *three books in one!* Uncle John went into the BRI vaults and gathered these great stories about creatures on the land, creatures in the sea, and creatures that go bump in the night. If you like whales, meerkats, ghosts, and weird people with hair all over their bodies, then sit down and get ready for hours of great bathroom reading.

Here's Part One of *Creature Feature*:

Wild & Woolly!

On behalf of the entire BRI staff, happy reading.

And, as Uncle John always says,

Go with the Flow!

CAN YOU HEAR ME NOW?

Meet Jack the basset hound from Fulda, Germany. He's got the longest dog ears in the world. And it's official: *Guinness World Records* measured them at 33.2 centimeters each—over a foot long! According to his owners, Claudia and Carsten Baus, Jack's ears flop into his food and water bowls. In fact, they're so long that this lovable one-year-old has a hard time keeping them off the ground and often trips over them when he walks.

RAT FACTS

A rat can fall from a five-story building without getting hurt.

A rat can survive without water longer than a camel.

A group of rats is called a *mischief*.

Rats care for the injured and sick in their group.

Rats can't vomit.

Rats sweat through the bottom of their feet.

A rat can tread water for three days.

Male rats are called *bucks*, females are called *does*, and babies are called *kittens*.

A rat's fur smells like grape soda.

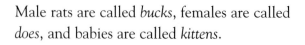

Rats pee as many as 80 times a day.

A rat can produce more than 25,000 droppings in a year.

A rat will grind its teeth when it's happy.

Rats can dive 100 feet underwater.

Rats' teeth grow five inches a year. They gnaw constantly to wear them down.

ZOMBIE DOG

This tale shows you can't keep a good dog down.

Sweetie was dead. Her owner, Glenda Stevens, was certain of it. Earlier in the day, she'd found the little dog's lifeless body sprawled across the road near the family's mailbox. Sweetie had been struck down by a delivery truck and her heart had stopped. Glenda was overcome with grief. She carried the limp body of the little dog to her backyard, dug a grave, and buried her.

Imagine Glenda's shock when hours later, she looked out of her back window and saw two hind legs sticking out of the ground. Sweetie was trying to dig her way out of her grave!

Glenda rushed to help her pet and then took her to the vet. The vet said the dog had a broken leg and a broken jaw and it would probably be best to put her to sleep. Glenda absolutely refused. Sweetie had already died once. Why make her go through that again?

Instead, she brought the dog to a specialist who was able to put Sweetie back together (just like in the movie *Frankenweenie*).

PETS OF THE FAMOUS (AND INFAMOUS)

If you ruled the world, what kind of pet would you have?

CLEOPATRA (69–30 B.C.). The queen of Egypt loved her cat, Charmian, so much that she designed her makeup to look like her cat's eyes.

KUBLAI KHAN (1215–1294). The Mongol emperor of China owned 5,000 mastiffs, the greatest number of dogs ever owned by one person.

NAPOLEON BONAPARTE (1769–1821). The emperor of France was deathly afraid of cats, but his wife Josephine had a pet orangutan that sat at her dinner table dressed in a coat.

PRESIDENT JOHN QUINCY ADAMS (1767–1848). He kept a pet alligator in the White House.

ADOLF HITLER (1889–1945). The Nazi dictator was scared of cats, but liked dogs. He had a German shepherd named Blondi that he trained to climb a ladder, jump through hoops, and sing.

DUMB ANIMAL TRICKS

Sometimes animals act just like humans…stupid.

OH, DEER!

The Storliens of Marietta, Minnesota, got the surprise of their life when they woke up one morning and found two "deer" lying in the front yard with their antlers locked together. One was a real deer, injured and struggling. The other was the Storliens' life-size concrete lawn ornament. Apparently the real deer spotted the fake deer during the night and challenged it to a duel. He charged, locked horns and knocked the lawn ornament over. Guess that showed him!

TRASH COMPACTOR

Did you hear about the bull terrier who swallowed a bottle cap, some Saran Wrap, a toy car, and some wire? The dog was rushed to the hospital, where doctors had to operate to remove the trash. In the recovery room the dog was put on an IV drip. When he woke up…he ate the IV tubing.

WHAT'S BLACK AND WHITE, BLACK AND WHITE, AND BLACK AND WHITE?

Answer: a herd of angry zebras kicking a minibus. The bus full of students was touring through a game park in Kenya when the enraged herd surrounded it and attacked. The driver finally got the kicking zebras to cool it by pouring bottles of water over the beasts' heads.

AND THE WINNER IS...

PICKIEST EATER. The Australian koala eats only eucalyptus leaves—and not from just *any* tree. It sorts through 500 species of eucalyptus to find one of the 36 types it likes. A pound and a half of eucalyptus leaves later, this fellow is full.

BIGGEST FARTER.
The regular old farm cow blasts out more than 105 pounds of methane gas a year. Count all the cows around the globe and that adds up to billions of pounds of gas. Talk about air pollution!

FASTEST RUNNER. The cheetah wins the gold medal, paws down, reaching a top speed of 70 miles an hour. Run, Spot, run!

SLOWEST MOVER. The three-toed sloth of South America wins this award with a land speed of six to eight feet a minute.

BIGGEST SLEEPYHEAD. The koala again. It snoozes for 22 hours a day. But the two-toed sloth is a close second, clocking 20 hours of z's a day.

SMALLEST MAMMAL. The Kitti's hog-nosed bat (also called the bumblebee bat) weighs a minuscule .07 ounces—about as much as a peanut!

DEADLIEST MAMMAL. Lion? Tiger? Cape buffalo? Hippo? Grizzly bear? Wrong on all counts. It's man.

WAGS TO RICHES

LUCKY DOG

Toby was a standard poodle who lived in a mansion in New York City. He slept on silk sheets on a miniature four-poster bed in his own bedroom. He even had a personal butler to serve his meals (his favorite: lamb chops). When his owner, Ella Wendel, died in 1931, she left her little darling $15 million. That's oodles for one poodle!

FAT CATS

When Dr. William Grier of San Diego, California, died, he left $415,000 to his 15-year-old cats Hellcat and Brownie. A third cat, Charlie Chan, got $250,000—all to himself.

STRONGHEART

Before there was a Lassie or an Air Bud,
he was the first great dog star.

In 1920 a Hollywood director and animal trainer named Lawrence Trimble discovered a German shepherd named Strongheart in Germany. Trimble took Strongheart home to try to turn him into a movie star.

Trimble was an unusual trainer. He didn't use treats as bribes to get Strongheart to perform. Instead, he read newspapers, books—even poetry—to the dog, and insisted that no one ever use baby talk with Strongheart or talk down to him. His training method was odd...but it worked.

At home Strongheart acted more like a human than a pet. He learned to help make his bed, arrange the furniture, put away his own toys, and even wash the car.

In 1921 he was ready for his first movie, *The Silent Call.* Strongheart became an instant star: thousands of fans would gather to see him when he toured the country. He made seven movies and was the biggest animal star of the 1920s. He even had a dog food named after him (it's still available today). Heading to Hollywood soon? Go to 1724 Vine Street. There you'll find a star on the Hollywood Walk of Fame...and all it says on it is "Strongheart."

ANIMAL CRACKERS

Two cows met in a field and started talking.

"Moo," said the first cow.

"I was just about to say the same thing!" said the second cow.

When his mother returned from the grocery store, little Jason pulled the box of animal crackers out of the bag and dumped them all over the kitchen counter.

"What on earth are you doing?" his mom asked.

"The box says you can't eat the cookies if the seal is broken," the boy explained. "I'm looking for the seal."

Q: How do you catch a runaway dog?
A: Hide behind a tree and make a noise like a bone!

Q: What do you call a chicken at the North Pole?
A: Lost.

Q: What is a twip?
A: A twip is what a wabbit takes when he wides on a twain.

Q: Why do cows wear bells?

A: Because their horns don't work.

Some kindergartners were on the playground when a fire truck zoomed past. Sitting in the front seat of the fire truck was a Dalmatian. The children started arguing about the dog's duties.

"They use him to keep the crowds back," said one kid.

"No," said another, "he's just for good luck."

A third kid brought the argument to a close. "You're both wrong. They use the dog to find the fire hydrant."

BIG KAHUNA!

Hippos in West Africa have come up with a cool way to travel—they surf! Every evening the hippos of Loango National Park in Gabon come out of the jungle and ride the breakers down the beach to the grasslands for dinner. After eating as much as 150 pounds each, they surf back up the beach to their sleeping grounds.

Experts guess the hippos take to the ocean because floating in the surf takes a big load off their feet—the average hippo weighs about 6,000 pounds!

WILD AND WOOLLY FACT

Hippos look like they're sweating blood. That's because they secrete a sticky pink liquid to protect their sensitive skin. It doubles as a sunblock and moisturizer.

BIG MOUTH

DID YOU KNOW?

• A hippo's head can weigh 1,000 pounds.

• A four-foot-tall child can stand up inside a hippo's open mouth.

• A hippo's eye can see above and below the water at the same time.

• A hippo's skin is so thick (1½ inches) that most bullets can't penetrate it.

MOST DANGEROUS ANIMAL IN AFRICA

Every year more people in Africa are killed by hippos than by all other animals combined. They're particularly

dangerous in rivers, where they capsize boats. A hippo can run twice as fast as a human and can cut a crocodile in half with a single bite!

ROCK-A-BYE BABY

Shh! Some pretty incredible things are happening in the wild nursery.

ZEBRAS are born with brown stripes.

PORCUPINES are born with soft quills (lucky for Mama)! The quills start to harden an hour after birth.

CAMELS are born without humps.

ELEPHANT babies suck their trunks the way baby humans suck their thumbs.

POLAR BEAR babies weigh only about one pound, yet they can grow to weigh as much as a car.

GIANT PANDA babies are the size of a stick of butter when they're born.

KANGAROO babies are smaller than your finger. The inch-long baby, called a *joey*, must crawl to its mother's pouch, where it will continue to grow into a fully developed baby kangaroo.

MOM OF THE YEAR

Lions eat gazelles, right? Not Kamuniak, an unusual lioness living in Samburu National Park in Kenya.

In 2002 Kamuniak turned the natural order of the animal world upside down when she adopted a baby oryx. An oryx is a type of gazelle and is usually the favorite dish of lions and other predators. But Kamuniak, who had no cubs of her own, began to lick and clean the orphaned oryx calf like a newborn cub. Worried rangers returned the calf to its mother. To their astonishment, Kamuniak promptly adopted another newborn oryx calf.

Kamuniak (which means "Blessed One" in the Samburu language) guards her calves from other lions and otherwise treats them like one of her own. So far she's adopted six in all. The baby gazelles stay with the lioness until they're strong enough to run away and rejoin their herd.

Meanwhile, Mama Kamuniak and her "babies" have become the most popular attraction at the game park, drawing visitors from all over the world.

SUPER DADS

Most baby animals are raised by their moms, but there are a few amazing dads in the animal kingdom.

TAMARINS win the title "Fathers of the Year," hands down. No other male animal takes care of its babies like these South American monkeys. Dad even helps Mom during labor. After the babies are born (she usually

has identical twins), he gently washes the little ones and returns them to their mother. For the first few weeks Dad takes care of Mom while she tends the kids. Then Dad takes over full-time, teaching them everything they need to know to survive. But he's careful to return them to their mother every few hours for meals.

RED FOXES are great fathers, too. They bring food to Mama fox while she nurses. When the pups get older, Dad teaches them how to forage by hiding food. He teaches them how to fight by playing. And when it's time for them to leave home, Dad kicks them out. But just in case Junior isn't ready to be on his own yet, he always leaves some extra food just outside the den. Way to go, Dad!

RUN WITH THE PACK

There are some very creative names for groups of animals. Can you guess them?

What do you call
a group of GIRAFFES?
a. rise
b. tower
c. stand

Answer: b. tower

What do you call
a group of TIGERS?
a. ambush
b. growl
c. gang

Answer: a. ambush

What do you call
a group of ZEBRAS?
a. pattern
b. herd
c. dazzle

Answer: c. dazzle

What do you call a
group of SQUIRRELS?
a. scurry
b. scramble
c. run

Answer: a. scurry

What do you call
a group of HIPPOS?
a. blob
b. bloat
c. flotilla

Answer: b. bloat

What do you call
a group of OTTERS?
a. mischief
b. romp
c. giggle

Answer: b. romp

What do you call
a group of RHINOS?
a. army
b. platoon
c. crash

Answer: c. crash

What do you call
a group of APES?
a. meeting
b. shrewdness
c. mob

Answer: b. shrewdness

ANIMAL CRACKERS

An elephant was drinking from a river when he spotted a turtle asleep on a log. The elephant ambled over and kicked the unsuspecting turtle across the river.

"Why did you do that?" asked a passing giraffe.

"Because I recognized it as the same turtle that took a nip out of my trunk 47 years ago."

"Wow, what a memory!" said the giraffe.

"Yep," said the elephant. "Turtle recall."

Earl: I just bought a pet zebra.
Pearl: What are you going to name him?
Earl: Spot.

Q: What do you call a well-dressed lion?
A: A dandy lion (dandelion).

Q: How does an elephant get down from a tree?
A: He sits on a leaf and waits till autumn!

Q: What do you get if you cross a leopard with a plum?
A: A spotted purple people eater!

Q: What did the judge say when he saw the skunk in the courtroom?
A: "Odor in the court!"

ZOO STORIES

Monkey See... A chimp named Feili spent too many hours people-watching at the zoo in Zhengzhou, China, and picked up a human habit that's really hard to kick—smoking. For years, Feili smoked all the cigarettes she could find on the ground. When she ran out, she begged visitors for more. If they said no, Feili flew into a screeching rage and spit on them. Happily, Feili finally kicked the habit in 2005.

Big Is Beautiful. Maggie is a 22-year-old African elephant at the Alaska Zoo who's fighting the battle of the bulge. She weighs 9,120 pounds—that's 3,000 pounds more than the average female elephant. Even with daily walks around the zoo, Maggie couldn't shed those extra pounds. So the zoo built Maggie her very own treadmill. Now she gets up in the morning and works out, just like her zookeepers.

DUMB DOG TRICKS

TEED OFF

A Labrador retriever named Meatball had a monstrous stomachache and was rushed to the vet for an emergency operation. Meatball, who should have been named Meathead, lived near a golf course…and had scarfed down a record 23 golf balls!

BRAIN FREEZE

In January 1935, a collie was stranded on a piece of ice on Lake Michigan. Rescuers tried to coax the dog to safety but she wouldn't budge… until they offered her some pork chops. She promptly dove into the freezing water and swam to shore, where she ate the pork chops. Then she jumped back into the icy lake and swam back to her iceberg!

STUCK ON YOU

Dempsey the Doberman had to have his jaws separated after he ate an entire tube of superglue.

FELIX THE CAT

Felix and his master, Thomas Lynan of St. Kilda, Australia, were inseparable. When the old man died, the black-and-white kitten was inconsolable. For five months, he hardly ate and spent his days and nights wandering the house looking for Mr. Lynan. Worried that Felix would die of grief, Lynan's daughter took the cat for a drive to cheer him up. When the car stopped at an intersection just outside of town, the cat, who had been lying limp in the back seat, suddenly leapt out the car window and ran off. The family searched everywhere for Felix but couldn't find him.

Days later, when Lynan's daughter went to visit her father's grave at Melbourne Cemetery ten miles away, she found Felix on the gravestone, marching back and forth like a sentry. She tried to take the cat home but he kept jumping out of the car and racing back to Lynan's grave. "In the end," she told a newspaper reporter, "we decided it would be kinder to let Felix stay behind."

Weeks later the reporter drove by the cemetery to see if Felix was still there. Sure enough, the black-and-white kitty was still standing guard over his master's grave.

HERE KITTY KITTY

A few cat facts to keep you feline fine.

MUMMY'S THE WORD

In ancient Egypt, cats were worshiped as gods. When they died, cats were mummified and taken to the temple of the cat god, Bastet. The Egyptians even mummified mice for the cats to take along as a snack in the afterworld.

DID YOU KNOW?

• A black cat is considered unlucky in America...but lucky in Great Britain.

• White cats with blue eyes are usually deaf.

MAMA CAT

The Weller family in Cranbook, British Columbia, woke up one morning to find their cat, Patches, nursing two baby mice. Patches already had seven kittens of her own. "I don't know where she found them," Mrs. Weller said, "but for some reason she brought them in instead of killing them." Good kitty.

LOOK OUT BELOW!

Gros Minou, a two-year-old orange-and-white cat from Quebec, holds the world record for surviving the longest fall. Gros Minou fell 200 feet off a 20th floor balcony into a flower bed. Amazingly, the lucky feline limped away with only a broken pelvis.

MISTER ED

A horse is a horse of course, of course, and no one can talk to a horse, of course. That is, of course, unless the horse is the famous Mr. Ed.

Mister Ed was a hit TV show in the 1960s that starred a "talking" horse named Mister Ed (his real name was Bamboo Harvester). This smart horse could do most of his own stunts, like opening the barn door and answering the telephone. What he *couldn't* do was talk. That was accomplished with a nylon bit which pulled his mouth open or by feeding him a peanut butter–like substance that made him chew.

Like many Hollywood stars, Ed could be difficult to work with. When he was tired, he'd just walk off the set. And when he got bored, he'd cross his back legs and yawn. When he was hungry, all shooting stopped while he strolled over to his bale of hay for a snack. That's star power!

⌒ WILD AND WOOLLY FACT ⌒ ⌒ ⌒ ⌒ ⌒⌒

On occasion Ed's stunt double was a zebra! ⌒

 # MORE RATS

ALL IN THE FAMILY

The San Carlos, California, health department got a call from horrified residents who reported seeing large rats eating the curtains in the window of a neighboring condo. Investigators found hundreds of rats running all over the house...even under the bedcovers. The owners's explanation: the rats were pets. "They have the bedrooms," the wife explained. "We sleep on the living room couch."

RAT TEMPLE

The Karni Mata temple in India is made of marble, gold, and silver. But it's known as the "Rat Temple." Why? It's home to about 20,000 rats who live there and run free through the place. Hindu monks feed them bowls of milk and sweets, and some people even drink from the rats' bowls! (It's considered good luck.) Want to go? You can...but be warned: shoes are not allowed!

PEST CONTROL, IRISH STYLE

In ancient Ireland, people believed rats could be "rhymed to death." It was thought that hearing poetry would whip the rats into such a frenzy that they'd kill each other.

RAT TO THE RESCUE

A West Virginia coal miner became pals with a rat he found down in the mines. He shared his food with the rat and always made sure it was out of the way before he set off any explosions in the tunnel. One day the rat began to act strangely. It scurried back and forth in front of the miner, first running to him and then disappearing around the corner. The miner set down his tools and followed the rat. Just as he turned the corner, the tunnel collapsed—right on the spot the miner had been standing only seconds before!

PAMPERED PETS

We already have dog parks, dog toys, and doggy day care. What will they come up with next?

WHAT'S FOR DINNER?

At the Three Dog Bakery they're serving Drooly Dream Bars, pup tarts, and carob-chip cookies. Sound good? Sorry—these tasty treats are for canine connoisseurs only. Gourmet dog treats are not just a passing fad; Three Dog Bakery has doggy diners throughout the United States, Canada, Japan, and Korea.

MEOW TV

At last! Television just for cats! Researchers say one third of all pet cats watch TV, so what could be better than *Meow TV*? This show brings shots of squirrels running up and down trees, inspirational programs about lions and tigers, and funny home videos of fellow felines right into your living room. *Purrfect!*

DOGS' DAY AT THE SPLASH

Hot dogs in Hutchinson, Kansas, get a chance to cool off on the last day of swim season at the Salt City Splash pool. People can go in the pool, too, but they have to stay in the shallow end. Dogs, however, can cannonball anywhere (and anyone) they like.

ANIMAL SIGNS

American Sign Language is a way to talk by using your hands. Can you match the sign with the animal's name?

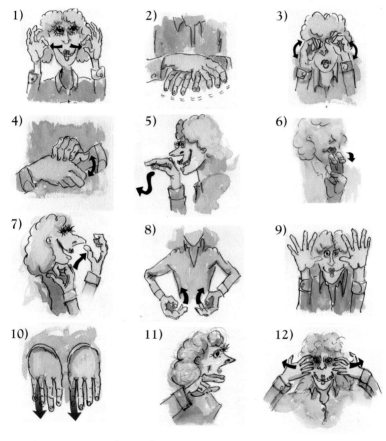

1)
2)
3)
4)
5)
6)
7)
8)
9)
10)
11)
12)

a. Tiger   **d.** Bird   **g.** Kangaroo   **j.** Snake

b. Cat   **e.** Elephant   **h.** Monkey   **k.** Spider

c. Deer   **f.** Giraffe   **i.** Owl   **l.** Turtle

SOLUTIONS

1) b; 2) k; 3) i; 4) l; 5) e; 6) j; 7) f; 8) h; 9) c; 10) g; 11) d; 12) a

41

WHAT ARE THEY?

MEERKATS!

DID YOU KNOW?

• Meerkats aren't cats—they're squirrel-sized mammals (related to the mongoose) that live in southern Africa.

• A meerkat's close-up vision is so bad that it often misses food that's right in front of it.

• When meerkats dig a tunnel, they form a line and pass dirt from one to the other, until it's out of the hole.

SUN WORSHIPPERS

When a meerkat gets chilly, it stands up on its hind
feet and faces the sun.
That's because the
dark skin on its belly
acts like a solar panel.
The meerkat even has
built-in sunglasses and
windshield wipers.
The dark band around
its eyes reduces the
harsh glare of the sun
and, every time a
meerkat blinks, a spe-
cial membrane on the
eye wipes away the
sand.

LIFE IN THE MOB

Belonging to a mob is critical for a meerkat—it could
never survive the African desert alone. The mob lives in
an elaborate underground home that has nurseries, sleeping rooms, and even a common toilet. To keep the mob
running smoothly, each meerkat has a specific job. There
are hunters, teachers, babysitters, diggers, and guards.

WILD & WOOLLY FACT

Meerkats can close their ears to keep dirt and sand out
while they are tunneling.

DING DONG!

One night Amelia Roybal of Albuquerque, New Mexico, answered her doorbell and discovered a very drunk monkey swaying on her doorstep. He staggered into the house, found her liquor cabinet, and poured himself a glass of whiskey. Amelia and her husband thought they were victims of a practical joke and

that someone was giving the monkey signals. But Myron the monkey was acting on his own.

After tossing back another shot of whiskey, Myron got belligerent and refused to give Mr. Roybal back the bottle. The Roybals called the sheriff, then cornered the monkey in the laundry room, where he promptly filled the washing machine full of soapsuds and flooded the room.

When the deputy sheriff arrived, he found Myron eating plastic fruit in the living room. Then Myron began hurling potatoes and oranges with dead-on accuracy at the Roybals and the deputy.

It took four more deputies and seven members of the Roybal family to capture the tipsy primate, but they finally did. It turned out Myron had escaped from a traveling circus. His trainer had started him drinking the hard stuff as a way to calm his nerves before performing. (Maybe somebody needs to train the trainer.)

AMAZING WORLD RECORDS

• **The Heaviest Dog.** Zorba, an English mastiff from London, tipped the scales at a whopping 343 pounds.

• **The Fattest Cat.** Himmy was a 46-pound tabby cat from Queensland, Australia, who was so chubby he had to be transported in a wheelbarrow.

• **The Oldest Dog.** Bluey was an Australian cattle dog who lived to the age of 29 years and 5 months.

WILD MEDICINE

Ever watch your dog eat grass when it's sick? It will sort through all the blades of grass to chew on the exact one that will give the best medicine. Other animals do the same thing.

CHIMPANZEES in Africa get rid of parasites by carefully folding the spiky leaves of the wild sunflower plant, rolling it around in their mouths, and swallowing it whole. Chimps hate the taste of it—they make faces when they eat—but apparently they know it helps them.

AFRICAN ELEPHANTS in western Kenya risk their lives to get to a cave in Mount Elgon just to chew on the mineral-rich rocks there. The sodium in this extinct volcano is essential for their health.

CAPUCHIN MONKEYS of Costa Rica rub them-selves with the Piper plant from the chili family to kill flies, ticks, and fleas and to numb the pain of insect bites.

RATS can't throw up. So when they're feeling sick, they eat clay—it absorbs the toxins in their stomachs.

GRIZZLY BEARS dig up the roots of the Loveroot plant (*Ligusticum porteri*), chew it to a pulp, and then rub the juices all over their faces and fur to treat stomachaches and bacterial infections.

PANDA-MONIUM

THE WEIGHTLIFTER

Ying Ying proves he is no "girly bear" during a performance in the Chinese Acrobats Arts Festival in Beijing. This 17-year-old is said to be the only panda who can lift weights, dunk a basketball, and drive a car.

BUFFALO PALS

Man's best friend comes in all shapes and sizes.

CHARLIE was a four-day-old orphan when he came to live with Roger Brooks and his wife, Veryl Goodnight, in Tesuque, New Mexico. Goodnight was a sculptor who needed a model for the buffalo piece she was working on. Charlie was a buffalo who needed a home.

In the beginning, Charlie was about the size of a golden retriever…and acted like one, too. He lived in the house, lounged on the sofa, and gave big wet kisses with his tongue. Even when he'd turned into a 200-pound bruiser, he tried to crawl into chairs with his owners.

"We weren't quite sure whether Charlie thought he was a human or whether he thought we were buffalo," Brooks says.

Being a buffalo, Charlie roamed wherever he pleased. Once he let himself into the house by walking through the screen door. He then marched up the stairs to the second floor and climbed into the king-size bed in the master bedroom.

As Charlie got older, Brooks felt the 400-pound furry beast should spend a little more time outdoors, so he often took the buffalo for walks into the hills (or rather, Charlie took *him*). Brooks would follow Charlie and depending on the buffalo's mood, they'd stroll or just stand still. It was up to Charlie to decide. "The old saying about buffalo is that you find out where they want to be," Brooks explained, "and then you put the fence around them."

Charlie, who eventually topped the scales at 1,800 pounds, was finally weaned from his indoor home and went to live outdoors with two other tame buffalo on Brooks' ranch.

BUFFY THE WATER BUFFALO

has been living with her family, the Bellingers, on their ranch near Humpty Doo, Australia, for over 18 years. Like most teenagers, Buffy is always hungry, gets in trouble a lot, and is really hard on the family car. She likes to rub her head up against the car (which puts dents in the hood). She won't stay outside because she hates the rain, so she lives inside with the Bellingers.

Her worst habit? Pulling freshly washed clothes off the line and chewing them. Buffy loves the taste of laundry soap, which probably makes the Bellingers wish they never heard the song that goes, "Oh, give me a home where the buffalo roam…"

OLD MACDONALD HAD A...

HORSES breathe only through their nostrils.

Twelve or more **COWS** are known as a *flink*.

GOATS' eyes have rectangular pupils.

PIGS have four toes on each hoof but only two touch the ground.

SHEEP can recognize as many as 50 other sheep by sight.

PIGS are very clean. They always poop away from where they live.

MULES always lift their tails before they bray.

The underside of a **HORSE'S** hoof is called a *frog*.

SHEEP have a built-in instinct to follow the lead ram. If a ram jumps over a stick and you take away the stick, every sheep after the ram will jump over the place where the stick was.

DONKEYS' eyes are set in their heads so they can see all four feet at once.

FAINTING GOATS

*This breed has bulging eyes and long, upright ears,
but otherwise they look and act like most goats.
Except for one teensy little problem...*

When fainting goats are startled, their muscles
stiffen and they fall over. The condition is called
myotonia. It can be so extreme in some goats that even
the noise of a passing car will make them keel over and
faint. After 10 or 15 seconds, the goat gets up and walks
away.

Shepherds used to keep fainting goats to protect their
sheep. If a wolf attacked the herd, the goat would faint,
which would attract the wolf and give the sheep a chance
to escape. So who would protect the goat? Guess he was
out of luck.

BOO!

THE NOSE KNOWS

POLAR BEARS can smell a seal on the ice 20 miles away. No wonder they're nicknamed "noses with legs."

ARCTIC HARES can smell dwarf willow leaves beneath several feet of snow.

SQUIRRELS can smell the tiny acorns they buried the previous autumn.

DOGS can smell one drop of urine in a swimming pool full of water.

WOLVES can smell prey more than a mile away if the wind is right. They can also smell the presence of an animal three days after it's left.

PIGS can be trained to find truffles—prized edible fungi that grow underground. (Some police departments use pigs to sniff out drugs.)

COONHOUNDS can smell when a raccoon's track was made, how fast it was traveling, and in what direction.

BLOODHOUNDS can follow a scent that is four days old.

DOGS can point out a sick catfish to fish farmers and even smell if there are termites in the house.

UDDERLY RIDICULOUS

MOO-SIC LOVERS

The municipal band of Cortina d'Ampezzo, Italy, was marching through town one day when a herd of 25 cattle suddenly broke out of their pasture and deliberately butted the band members to the ground. Then, to everyone's surprise, the cattle stood around affectionately licking the instruments.

BEASTLY
EXPRESSIONS

Where does Grandma come up with the crazy phrases she uses? Here are the origins of three of them.

DON'T LET 'EM GET YOUR GOAT.

Meaning: Don't let them upset you.

Story: Racehorses and other high-strung Thoroughbreds are sometimes given goats as stall-mates. The goats seem to calm the horses down, especially before a big race. At one time, crooks who were betting against a horse would steal its goat as a way to upset the horse and make it lose the race.

WHO LET THE CAT OUT OF THE BAG?

Meaning: Who revealed the secret?

Story: In medieval days, piglets were taken to markets and sold in sacks. Some crooks would stuff a cat into the bag and try to pass it off as a piglet. If the cat escaped in front of the potential buyer, so did the secret.

HE'S A STOOL PIGEON.

Meaning: He's a traitor.

Story: Pigeon hunters would use tame birds, tied to stools, to lure wild pigeons to come close and be caught.

AND THE WINNER IS...

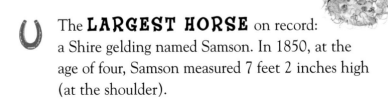

⋃ The **LARGEST HORSE** on record: a Shire gelding named Samson. In 1850, at the age of four, Samson measured 7 feet 2 inches high (at the shoulder).

⋃ Samson was also the **HEAVIEST HORSE** on record. He weighed 3,360 pounds.

⋃ The **SMALLEST PONY** in history was a stallion named "Little Pumpkin." He stood 14 inches tall and weighed only 20 pounds.

⋃ The **OLDEST HORSE** on record: an English barge horse named "Old Bill." A horse's typical life span is 25 years. Bill was 62 when he died in 1802.

⋃ The **LONGEST TAIL** was on an American palomino named Chinook. It was 22 feet long.

⋃ The **LONGEST MANE** was 18 feet long and grown by a California mare named Maude.

⋃ The **FASTEST PONY EXPRESS RIDE** was 7 days, 17 hours—it was carrying President Lincoln's inaugural address.

ANIMAL NEWS
HAM ON THE LAM!

In 1998 two red-haired pigs escaped from a slaughterhouse in the town of Tamworth, England, by squeezing through a fence and swimming across the icy Avon River.

The British dubbed them "Butch Cassidy and the Sundance Pig" after the famous Wild West outlaws.

For the next six days TV crews and helicopters searched the countryside for the two escaped swine.

The huge outpouring of support for the runaway piggies gave their owner a change of heart—he spared their lives and sold them to a London newspaper for the rumored sum of $24,500. The famous porkers were finally placed in an animal sanctuary and immortalized in a BBC television movie, *The Legend of the Tamworth Two.*

AND SPEAKING OF PIGS...

In the 1800s, families used to spend most of their money on a pig. Their pig acted as a garbage can by eating all the family's food scraps and also gave them pork, bacon, and sausage. When asked if he had any money, a farmer would reply, "No. All my money's in the pig." When people stopped keeping pigs they made a replica of their pig to put their money in. Hence the practice of saving money in a...

...PIGGY BANK.

ANIMALS TO THE RESCUE

TRIXIE THE NURSE. Jack Fyfe of Sydney, Australia, lived alone, with only his border collie, Trixie, for company. So when he woke up one morning to discover he'd suffered a paralyzing stroke during the night, he thought he was a goner. He knew it might be days before anyone would find him. To his amazement, Trixie took care of him. The collie brought him water by soaking a towel in her water bowl and draping it over his face. After her bowl ran dry, Trixie soaked the towel in the toilet. The faithful dog kept Fyfe alive for nine days, staying by his side until his relatives finally found him and got him to a hospital.

CAT ATTACK. Bringing the family cat along on vacation saved two-year-old Janey Kraven's life. Janey was playing in front of her family's Adirondack Mountains cabin when a black bear seized her in its jaws and shook her like a rag doll. Jasper the cat sprang onto the bear's head and scratched at its eyes. The enraged bear let go of Janey and chased the cat into the woods. When Jasper came home two hours later, unharmed, he received a hero's welcome.

MAD COWS

PLANE SILLY

A British couple who left their antique airplane in a pasture while they went to lunch had a rude awakening when they returned. While they were chowing down at the local pub in Hereford, England, a herd of cows was enjoying their own meal: the airplane. Apparently the cows really liked the taste of the old canvas covering the vintage plane's metal frame. Those cows had expensive taste—their meal cost $15,000.

NIGHT-NIGHT

A farmer in Syracuse, New York, has discovered a way to keep his milk cows happy and producing lots of milk: water beds. John Marshman put several water beds in his barn...and the cows love sleeping on them. "Sometimes the cows stand in line and wait for a cow to leave," he said, "just so they can get in the same water bed."

GIRAFFE-A-MANIA

In 1827 a giraffe named Zarafa came to Paris as a gift to King Charles X. The French, most of whom had never seen such a creature, went wild for it, calling it "Sweet Thing." More than 100,000 people came to visit Zarafa and suddenly giraffe furniture, porcelain, and decorations were everywhere. Ladies wore gowns with themes like "Giraffe in love" and "Giraffe in exile." Men tied "giraffe knots" in their ties. Most bizarre was the "à la giraffe" hairdo. It was so tall that the women who wore it had to sit on the floor of their carriages when they went out to a ball.

DID YOU KNOW?

• An adult giraffe can easily look into a second story window.

• A giraffe's neck can be six feet long but has only seven bones—just like a human's.

• A giraffe can clean its ears with its tongue. (Can you?)

TALKING TREES

A giraffe's favorite food is the thorny acacia tree. It would strip a tree bare if the tree didn't have a clever way to stop the giraffe from overeating. Once the animal begins nibbling its leaves, the acacia tree broadcasts a warning—like a chemical SOS—to the rest of the tree to move a bitter-tasting chemical called *tannin* from its roots and branches into its leaves. The tannin makes the leaves taste terrible, even to a giraffe. But the giraffe can't just move on to another tree. The tree that was being munched on also warns nearby trees by sending a chemical warning into the air. Once the alarm is sounded, it takes less than 30 minutes for all of the trees in the grove to fill their leaves with tannin. The giraffes have learned that the best way to eat their favorite food is to just nibble a little bit and then move to another grove.

WILD AND WOOLLY FACT

The giraffe is one of the few animals born with horns. The horns lie flat against the skull when it is born and pop up during the giraffe's first week of life.

GOING APE!

Life behind bars made this gang go a little stir crazy.

In 1994 the baboons at the Emmen Zoo in Holland—all 120 of them—suddenly climbed into the trees in their compound and refused to come down. The zookeepers

were baffled. The hamadryas baboons normally spent most of their time on the ground, but now they would come out of the trees only for dinner, and even then, they'd grab the food and race back to the treetops to eat. This continued for three days. Then suddenly, they came out of the trees and acted as if nothing had happened. What caused their three-day climbing expedition? No one knows for sure…but it did coincide exactly with the collision of Jupiter and the comet Shoemaker-Levy.

WILD AND WOOLLY FACT

The ancient Egyptians considered hamadryas baboons to be the sacred attendants of Thoth, the scribe (writer) of the gods.

WASSUP?

Most animals can't talk, but hey, who needs words?

CHIMPANZEES greet each other by touching hands.

AN ADULT LION sends out messages with a roar that can be heard up to five miles away.

WHEN TWO DOGS approach each other, the one that wags its tail slowly is the dominant dog.

ELEPHANTS "hear" super-low frequency calls from other elephants over a mile away through the bottoms of their feet.

CATS meow at humans but rarely at each other.

GORILLAS stick out their tongues when they're angry.

THE ONLY KIND OF DOG that can't bark is a basenji. It can, however, yodel.

AND THE WINNER IS...

TOP FIVE HEAVIEST LAND MAMMALS (AVERAGE WEIGHT)

1. African elephant (16,500 lbs.)
2. Hippo (9,900 lbs.)
3. White rhino (8,000 lbs.)
4. Giraffe (4,200 lbs.)
5. Bison (2,200 lbs.)

TOP TEN DOG NAMES

1. Sam 2. Max
3. Lady 4. Bear
5. Buddy 6. Maggie
7. Bailey 8. Jake
9. Molly 10. Sadie

TOP TEN LONGEST-LIVING LAND ANIMALS (AVERAGE LIFESPAN)

1. Box turtle (100 years)
2. Human (80)
3. African elephant (40)
4. Grizzly bear (25)
5. Horse (20)
6. Gorilla (20)
7. Polar bear (20)
8. White rhino (20)
9. Black bear (18)
10. Lion (15)

TOP FOUR FASTEST MAMMALS

1. Cheetah (71 mph)
2. Antelope (57 mph)
3. Wildebeest (50 mph)
4. Lion (50 mph)

THE GREAT ESCAPE

Never underestimate an animal's resourcefulness.

The plan was simple: first he'd paddle across the water-filled moat, using a log as a raft. Then he'd climb the cement wall, grab a bicycle, and pedal away. Unfortunately for Juan, a spectacled bear at the Berlin Zoo, the bicycle was chained to a bike rack and it wasn't going anywhere. But that didn't dampen Juan's fun. He ambled away from the bike and spent half an hour frolicking on the zoo's playground. While excited visitors snapped photos of Juan's Day Out, nervous zookeepers shot him with tranquilizers.

Though some parents were really concerned about their children's safety, the zoo's deputy director wasn't worried. "Spectacled bears eat both vegetables and meat," he said, "but children do not tend to be on their menu. I'd have been a lot more worried if one of our polar bears had escaped."

YOU BETTER RUN!

If a **STRIPED SKUNK** does a handstand...
Look out—it's spray time!

If a **GRIZZLY BEAR** stands on its hind legs and puffs its cheeks...
It's the grizzly way of saying, "My next meal is...you."

If a **MUSK OX** bows its head and presses its nose against its knee...
This action releases a smelly liquid from a gland in its nose (musk!) and means this ox is about to stomp on you.

If you hear a **LEOPARD** cough...
It's probably the last sound you'll ever hear, because that's what leopards do right before they pounce.

If a **CAPE BUFFALO** starts smashing bushes with its horns...
It's giving you a little demonstration of what it's going to do to your head.

If a
CHIMP
stops
grinning
at you...
*Lips pressed
together
tightly means
he's about to
play a serious
game of
tag—and
you're it.*

If a **BLACK RHINO** starts bouncing around like it's had too much caffeine...
Here it comes—the animal equivalent of a runaway train.

If a **FEMALE LION** flicks her tail briskly from side to side while she stares at you...
Uh-oh. She's decided to have you for lunch.

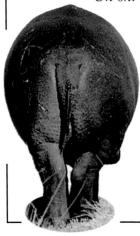

If a **HIPPO** turns his butt toward you and starts wagging his tail like a windshield wiper...
He's about to give you a dung shower— that's the male hippo's messy but oh-so-effective way of marking his territory.

LOOK WHO'S TALKING

Match the animal with its sound.

1. bear	**a.** gibbers
2. fox	**b.** snorts
3. giraffe	**c.** barks
4. ape	**d.** roars
5. hippopotamus	**e.** trumpets
6. lion	**f.** howls
7. elephant	**g.** bellows
8. rhinoceros	**h.** bleats
9. wolf	**i.** growls
10. bull	**j.** brays

ANSWERS

1-i (bears growl); 2-c (foxes bark); 3-h (giraffes bleat); 4-a (apes gibber); 5-j (hippos bray); 6-d (lions roar); 7-e (elephants trumpet); 8-b (rhinos snort); 9-f (wolves howl); 10-g (bulls bellow)

ROYAL RIDES

THE GREAT HORSE

Alexander the Great conquered most of the known world (Europe and Asia) in the 4th century B.C. According to legend, he always rode into battle astride his black stallion, Bucephalus. Alexander's father had owned the horse but could never tame it. Ten-year-old Alexander realized that the horse was afraid of its own shadow, so he turned Bucephalus to face the sun. Once it couldn't see its shadow, it relaxed, and Alexander began to train it.

Together, the duo traveled 11,000 miles in eight years. When Bucephalus died at the age of 30, Alexander named a town in Pakistan in his horse's honor.

NO HORSE SENSE

The Roman emperor **Caligula** (A.D. 12–41) had a horse named Incitatus who lived in a marble stable with an ivory stall and purple blankets. Incitatus often wore a jeweled collar and had his own house with furniture and slaves.

HORSE SHOES?

Julius Caesar's favorite horse had hooves that looked like human feet. Each hoof was split in five parts that resembled toes. When the colt was born, soothsayers predicted, "The master of this horse will one day rule the world." Caesar made sure he became the master.

ANIMALS TO THE RESCUE

➕ ➕

BACKSEAT DRIVER

A schnauzer named Bitsy was in the passenger seat when her owner suffered a heart attack while speeding down a Texas freeway. Bitsy quickly turned the wheel so the car would leave the road and then bit her owner, Jesus Martinez, until his foot came off the accelerator. The car stopped safely on the side of the road and Martinez recovered in the hospital.

CALL 911

Lyric the Irish setter was trained to help Judy Bayly, who had asthma. Once when Bayly's oxygen mask fell off during an asthma attack, Lyric knocked the phone off the hook and actually dialed the emergency number, saving Bayly's life.

GOOD DOGGIE!

FOREVER FAITHFUL

A bronze statue in Togliatti, Russia, honors the memory of a remarkably loyal German shepherd. When his owners were killed in a car crash, Faithful refused to move from the spot where they died. Townspeople brought Faithful food and water and tried to coax him into their homes, but the dog lived up to his name. He remained faithful to his owners until he died seven years later of old age.

BREEDS APART

Newfoundland dogs are strong swimmers. Why? They have webbed feet.

The greyhound has the best eyesight of any dog breed.

Great Danes can eat up to $8\frac{1}{2}$ pounds of food a day.

Chinese crested dogs can get acne.

HOW OLD IS YOUR DOG?

Want to figure out your dog's true age in people years?

1. Count the first full year as 15 years.
2. Count the second full year as 10 years.
3. Count all of the following years as 3 years apiece.

So a 5-year-old dog would be:
15 + 10 + 3 + 3 + 3 = 34 years old

RAILROAD JACK

*One of South Africa's most famous signalmen
wasn't a man—he was a baboon.*

I n 1877 a railroad worker in South Africa named
James Wide accidentally fell under a train and lost
both of his legs. Without the use of his legs he could no
longer work on the trains, so he became a signalman at
Uitenhage Station near Port Elizabeth. His job: using a
system of flags and flashing lights to signal trains to slow
down or stop. Then he would pull a lever to transfer
them to different tracks.

Wide lived all alone near the station, struggling to
get around on peg legs and crutches. One day he saw a
trained baboon named Jack at a market in Uitenhage.

Hoping the baboon might help him, Wide brought Jack home and they soon became fast friends. As time passed, Jack began to do chores around the house: pumping water, doing dishes, and working in the garden. Soon the baboon learned to help Wide at the railroad station, too.

Locomotive drivers would blow four whistle blasts when they needed coal. Wide would hobble out on his crutches and hand them the key to the coal shed. One day Jack the baboon heard the whistle…and immediately raced to give the key to the locomotive driver. Soon, Jack was not only delivering keys but also giving the signals to the engineers and pulling the levers to switch the tracks. Jack did his job so well that the government gave him an employment number and a monthly paycheck.

"Jack the Signalman" worked at his job for 13 years… and never made a single mistake.

OTHER WORKING ANIMALS

ASTRONAUT: Laika was the world's first space traveler. Russian scientists shot the small dog into orbit in a satellite called Sputnik II on November 3, 1957.

GUIDE DOG: The first guide dogs—German shepherds— were trained by the German government to assist blind war veterans at the end of World War I.

LAB ASSISTANT: Rats' keen sense of smell can detect diseases like tuberculosis and bladder cancer in laboratory samples. A rat can diagnose up to 2,000 lab samples a day; a human (using a microscope) can only diagnose 20.

'ROO

You'll find these critters in Australia.

DID YOU KNOW?

- There are 45 kinds of kangaroos, including wallabies, walleroos, and pademelons.

- Male kangaroos are called *boomers*; females are *flyers*.

- If you lift a kangaroo's tail off the ground it can't jump.

- Kangaroos can go for months without water.

- A group of kangaroos is called a *mob*.

1-2 PUNCH

Kangaroos really do punch at each other when they fight. One prizefighting kangaroo escaped from a Japanese zoo and knocked out three men before two policemen who knew judo finally stopped him.

THE ONE-EYED KANGAROO

The true story of an Australian hero.

In 1993 Lulu the kangaroo was found wounded in the pouch of her mother, who'd been killed by a car. The Richards family adopted the one-eyed western gray, and she quickly became one of the family, acting more like a dog than a kangaroo. As Mr. Richards worked around his ranch, Lulu was always at his side.

While he was out inspecting damage from a bad storm, a branch fell on Richards and knocked him out. Lulu immediately tried to alert the family. Standing guard over the injured man, she barked like a dog until the family came running out to see what was wrong.

According to Richards, "If it wasn't for Lulu, I'd be pushing up daisies." Her behavior was so extraordinary that Lulu became the first native animal to receive Australia's National Animal Valor Award.

ANIMAL CRACKERS

One day an arctic explorer came face to face with a polar bear. Afraid of being eaten, he fell to his knees and started praying. When the bear knelt down beside him and started praying too, the man shouted, "It's a miracle! I'm saved!"

The polar bear opened one eye and said, "Shh! Please don't talk while I'm saying grace."

What do you get if you cross a flea with a rabbit?
Bugs Bunny.

How do you stop a skunk from smelling?
Hold its nose.

What do you get from a cow at the North Pole?
Ice cream.

Why do mother kangaroos hate rainy days?
Because the kids have to play inside.

What do you call a flying ape?
A hot-air baboon.

What kind of beans do llamas like to eat?
Llima beans.

Q: WHAT IS IT???

Its nose is billed like a duck's.

 It lays eggs like a chicken.

It has poisonous venom like a snake.

 It has sharp claws for digging like a mole.

It has waterproof fur like a seal.

 It has a flat tail like a beaver.

Its feet are webbed like an otter's.

When the first specimens of this Australian mammal were brought to England in 1798, the British thought it was a fake. What is it?

Answer on the next page.

A: IT'S A PLATYPUS!

As odd as it looks, the duck-billed platypus is perfectly suited to live underwater and underground.

The bill. The platypus's bill isn't hard like a bird's beak—it's made of soft cartilage, like your nose or ears. The bill is lined with tiny sensors that help the platypus find food in dark places.

Babies. The duck-billed platypus lays eggs. Each egg is less than an inch long and sticks to the fur on the mother's belly. The babies, called *platypups*, hatch after ten days and stay stuck to their mom until they are three to four months old. Only two other mammals lay eggs (they're both in the anteater family).

Claws. When the male platypus is attacked it protects itself by clawing at its enemy with the spurs on its hind legs. Those spurs really pack a punch—they're filled with poisonous venom that's strong enough to kill a dog.

Habitat. You can find this weird and wonderful beast along the banks of freshwater rivers and lakes in Eastern Australia.

MORE ZOO STORIES

Hey! Stop monkeying around!

SLIP AND SLIDE

At the Oklahoma Zoo the keepers had just finished mopping the floor of the orangutan's cage when the ape, who was sulking in the corner, stood up with his hands out, palms down, took a running start, and slid across the floor, as if he were surfing.

PLAYING WITH BONGO

It seems there's a practical joker in every crowd, even at the Sacramento Zoo. When Brigette, a slightly pudgy gorilla, got stuck in a rubber tub in her cage, her mate Bongo rushed to her side—not to help her, but to tickle her. As Brigette struggled to get out of the tub and away from his tickling, Bongo and their son Fossey collapsed on the floor in laughter.

GOING APE

Zippy was a spirited chimp from New Orleans who decided to sneak out of his owner's house and have a night on the town. Hours later, the police found him riding around in a van with four teenagers. The teenagers said they'd found Zippy outside a convenience store. He was wearing tennis shoes and blue underwear, and smoking a cigar.

HOLLYWOOD HOUNDS

LASSIE starred in nine movies, a radio show that lasted six years, and a TV series that ran for 19 years.

Lassie is supposed to be a girl, but all of the dogs who have played her were males.

There have been nine Lassies.

The original Lassie was named Pal. He made seven *Lassie* movies from 1947 to 1951, and starred in the first TV episode of *Lassie* at the age of 14.

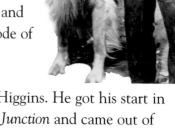

BENJI'S real name was Higgins. He got his start in the '60s TV show *Petticoat Junction* and came out of retirement at age 14 to star in the Benji movies.

TOTO in *The Wizard of Oz* was a cairn terrier named Terry. He got the part because he looked just like the dog in the pictures from the book.

RIN TIN TIN had been rejected by every studio in Hollywood when Warner Bros., a studio that was about to go broke, took a chance on him in 1922. The success of his movies saved the studio.

FRAIDY PIGGY

Ever wonder what's hiding under the bed or in the closet? It probably never occurred to you to wonder what's going to come in through the back door.

An elderly couple in Minden, Germany, had just settled in for the night when a wild boar crashed through their patio door and jumped in bed with them. "I thought a bomb had dropped," said Andreas Janik, 71. "I sat up and there was a wild pig in bed, tusks and all." The pig was being chased by a neighbor's Yorkshire terrier. The Janiks had to chase the dog off before they could get the pig to leave. "I can't believe it was afraid of such a little dog."

I VANT TO SUCK YOUR BLOOD!

VAMPIRE BATS aren't dangerous to people. How-ever, if you're a cow, a pig, or a horse—look out. These three-inch-long bats attack while their victims are asleep. They land near the animal, then crawl over the ground and try to find a furless part of the body, like an ankle or the neck. Finally they make a small slit-like wound in the animal and suck out the blood. A vampire bat drinks more than its own weight in blood every night.

GHOST PETS

Man's best friend is a…ghost?

PET CEMETERY

If late one night you happen to be passing the Hollywood Cemetery in Richmond, Virginia, stop and listen closely. You might hear the happy barks of ghost pets scampering around their owner's grave. The people of Richmond say they belong to author Ellen Glasgow who left orders to have her dogs exhumed from her backyard and buried with her when she died.

GHOSTLY WARNING

Norma Kresgal was sound asleep in her home in New York when the barking of her collie, Corky, suddenly awakened her. But that wasn't possible. Corky was dead! Yet his warning was so vivid that she got up to see what was the matter and discovered that her house was on fire. Her dead pet had saved her life.

NOW YOU SEE HIM, NOW YOU DON'T

At King John's Hunting Lodge in Somerset, England, a tabby cat enters a wood-paneled room through a closed door, curls up happily on the rug, and then…disappears.

THE BEAR FACTS

How can such a fierce creature be so cute?
Fortunately, you'll never bump into a polar
bear...unless you live near the North
Pole (or go to the zoo).

DID YOU KNOW?

• A polar bear is the only
mammal with hair on the
soles of its feet.

• Polar bears are the
tallest bears (10 feet).

• All polar bears
are left-handed.

• Polar bears
don't drink
water.

WHITE OUT

Polar bears are white, right? Wrong. A polar bear's fur is made of hollow, colorless hairs that transmit ultraviolet rays to the bear's skin and reflect the light. This makes for great camouflage. When a polar bear stalks its prey, it hides its black nose with its paw or covers it in snow so it will completely blend in with its environment.

It doesn't always work out, though. At the San Diego Zoo, three polar bears turned green when an algae colony moved into their hair shafts. Zookeepers brought back their white appearance with a little water and a lot of salt.

WILD AND WOOLLY FACT

Polar bears can swim 60 miles without stopping. They swim with only their front paws—they hold their back legs straight out to steer.

FROZEN FOODS

*Cool food facts from the
far, frozen North.*

BEAR SHARE

• The Siberian brown bear eats only fish heads and throws away the bodies.

• The Siberian white-breasted bear eats only the fish bodies and throws away the heads.

OFF WITH THEIR HEADS!

The Arctic fox bites the heads off birds before burying them for their winter reserves.

ARCTIC ANTI-FREEZE

Most animals don't eat moss because it's hard to digest and has little nutritional value. But reindeer love it. Why? It has a special chemical that keeps the reindeer's body fluids from freezing, just like antifreeze keeps water in cars from freezing.

Q: WHY DON'T POLAR BEARS EAT PENGUINS?

Penguins live in the Southern Hemisphere—Antarctica, Australia, New Zealand, and South America. But polar bears live only in the Northern Hemisphere—northern Canada, Russia, and the Arctic Circle.

HISTORY MAKERS

It's reigning cats and dogs!

KING CANINE. In the 11th century, the king of Norway took revenge on his subjects—who had once ousted him—by putting his dog, Saur, on the throne. The dog reigned for three years.

CAT-ASTROPHE. The Battle of Agincourt (1415) was one of England's greatest triumphs. Led by King Henry V, the English defeated a much larger French army. How? They brought cats into battle to keep rats away from their food, but the French didn't. Legend has it that the night before the big battle, rats got into the French armory and gnawed through the archers' bow-strings. When the battle was fought, the French had no arrow power and King Henry—and his cats—won.

DOG EXPLORES AMERICA. From 1803 to 1806, explorers Lewis and Clark mapped the western United States with the help of Seaman, a 150-pound Newfoundland. The pooch was a respected member of the expedition team who warned them of charging buffalo and bears. His adventures were reported in the explorers' diaries and in the book *The Captain's Dog*.

BIG SCAREDY-CAT. The ancient Greek conqueror Alexander the Great was so afraid of cats that he would faint at the sight of one.

LION TALES

Knights of old often put images of lions on their shields and flags. Every pose had a French name, because French was the language of chivalry.

1. *Lion rampant* (raised forepaws)
2. *Lion statant guardant* (standing, full face)
3. *Lion rampant guardant* (raised forepaws, full face)
4. *Lion passant* (walking, right leg raised)
5. *Lion statant* (standing)
6. *Lion passant guardant* (walking, full face)
7. *Lion sejant* (sitting)
8. *Lion sejant rampant* (sitting up on forelegs)
9. *Lion couchant* (lying down)
10. *Lion salient* (leaping)
11. *Lion coward* (tail between legs)
12. *Lion queue fourchée* (double tailed)

NAME THAT HORSE

APPALOOSA. This type of spotted horse, first bred

by the Nez Perce tribe in Oregon and Washington, was originally called "a Palouse horse" after the Palouse River. That became "a Palousey," then "Appaloosey," and finally, Appaloosa.

MORGAN. As partial payment of a debt, in 1790 a one-year-old colt was given to a Vermont schoolteacher named Justin Morgan. The colt was the founding sire of the Morgan breed—pony-sized with large eyes and a white stripe down the center of the face.

CLYDESDALE. These large draft horses (horses used for pulling heavy loads) with fringed hooves were named after Scotland's Clydesdale district. They are probably best known as the team that pulls the Budweiser beer wagon in TV commercials and parades.

PERCHERON. In 1823 a horse named Jean Le Blanc was born in the Perche region of France, and all of today's Percheron bloodlines trace directly to this horse. Originally the Percheron were used to carry knights into battle; now they are draft animals.

LIPIZZAN. In 1580 Archduke Charles II of Austria established a stud farm in Lipizza (now known as Lipica, Slovenia). He imported the best Spanish, Andalusian, Barbs, and Berber horses and bred them with the local Karst horse. The result is the famous leaping white Lipizzan stallions.

MUSTANG. The Spanish brought these horses to Mexico in the 16th century, but many of them escaped and headed north. They soon formed herds and roamed the western plains of the United States. The word *mustang* comes from the Spanish *mesteno* which means "stray or riderless horse."

ARABIAN. Considered by many horse lovers to be the finest breed, the Arabian has been bred for centuries by the Bedouin people of Syria, Iran, Iraq, and the Arabian peninsula.

WILD AND WOOLLY FACT

The smallest horse breed is the Falabella—a miniature from Argentina. The tallest of the breed stands less than 34 inches at the shoulder.

ANIMAL NEWS

CATS PREDICT EARTHQUAKE!

According to James P. Berkland, a geologist from California, there are many ways to predict earthquakes. When he predicted the 1989 Loma Prieta quake, he studied the tides and positions of the sun and moon. But he also studied the number of lost cat ads in the local papers. After ten full years of scientific observation, Berkland concluded that "cats tend to vanish just before a major tremor."

Is he right? In 1976 the people in the northern Italian village of Friuli noticed that their cats were acting strangely. Many of them were running around scratching on doors and howling to get out. Once out, they raced to get out of town. Three hours later the area was hit by a major earthquake.

WAR HEROES

They're trained to recognize booby traps and land mines, warn troops of ambushes, and even sacrifice their lives to save their "fellow soldiers."

CHIPS

When this U.S. Army dog and his handler, Private John Rowell, landed in Sicily in 1943, they were pinned down on the beach by a hail of machine-gun fire from an enemy bunker. Then Chips, a German shepherd–husky mix,

shook off his leash and charged. The enemy soldiers sprayed bullets at the attacking dog, nicking his shoulder and putting one in his hip. But nothing stopped Chips. He tore into the bunker and, moments later, four terrified enemy soldiers surrendered. One of them still had Chips clamped solidly onto his neck. Chips was awarded the Silver Star for bravery and a Purple Heart for wounds received in action. Disney even made a TV movie about Chips in 1990, called *Chips the War Dog*.

GANDER

This Newfoundland dog fought with Canadian troops against the Japanese during World War II. During a fierce battle on Christmas Eve in 1941, some Canadian soldiers lay wounded on the field when the enemy lobbed a live grenade at them. Gander picked up the grenade and carried it away. The dog was killed instantly when it exploded. "Was it a dog playing a dog game? I don't think so," said Jeremy Swanson of the Canadian War Museum. "Gander had seen many grenades explode in the days leading up to that moment. He saw something dangerous and took it away from his friends." Gander received the Silver Medal for bravery under fire.

SORTER

Two thousand years ago in ancient Greece, invaders used the cover of darkness to mount a sneak attack on the citadel of Corinth. What the attackers didn't know was that the Corinthians had set 50 watchdogs on guard along the seashore. When the invaders stepped out of their boats, the dogs set on them like lions. The outnumbered dogs fought bravely until all were killed but one—Sorter. He ran back into town, barking a warning that gave the Corinthians time to mount a defense and repel the invaders. The people were so grateful that they raised a monument to honor Sorter and the 49 loyal dogs who died that day.

DUMB DOG TRICKS

BAD HAIR DAY

The police were called in when a French woman's guard dog refused to let her into her own home. She'd gone to the beauty parlor and her new hairdo changed her looks so much that the dog didn't recognize her.

MOBILE MEAL

What do you do when you can't find your cell phone? Dial the number and listen for the ring. That's what a gas station attendant in Turkey did...and was shocked to hear his dog's stomach ringing! Apparently his pup had swallowed his Nokia.

ANIMALS TO THE RESCUE

BABY ON BOARD

A woman in Raducaneni, Romania, nearly fainted when her sheepdog came home with a newborn baby. She was afraid the pooch, Vasile, had stolen the child from someone's home. But actually, Vasile had found the baby abandoned in a field two miles away. The dog carried the child home in his mouth, then barked and scratched at the door until someone came to help.

HEAD 'EM UP

In 1996 a farmer in Carmarthen, Wales, was tending a sick calf when a neighbor's bull attacked him. The bull beat Donald Mottram senseless, stomping on his head and body until he lost consciousness. When he came to later, he found that his cows had formed a protective circle around him. Led by Daisy, the "bell cow" of the herd, the cows kept up an impenetrable shield against the raging bull, which charged them over and over but never broke through their ranks. Finally the farmer was able to crawl for help. When asked to explain why his cows came to his defense, Mottram said, "I have always treated the animals reasonably and in return, they have looked after me."

WHO LET THE DOG OUT?

Here's one pooch who doesn't wait for a car ride when he feels the need for speed.

BOARDER BULLDOG

Tyson is an English bulldog from Huntington Beach, California, who loves to skateboard. This major boarder taught himself how to skate when he was just one year old. He runs with three paws on the road and steers with his fourth paw on the skateboard. When Tyson gets going fast enough, he hops on the board and skates like a pro.

MORRIS THE CAT

T he year was 1968. Morris the Cat was moments away from execution in a Chicago animal shelter when animal handler Bob Martwick spotted him and saw right away that this tabby cat had star quality. He took Morris from the shelter, straight to Hollywood. Soon the 9Lives cat food company made Morris the "finicky eater" star of their TV commercials. Morris became the darling of the talk-show circuit, starring in the movie *Shamus* with Burt Reynolds, hosting his own TV special, and even "co-authoring" three books on cat care. But the tough tabby from Chicago never forgot his roots—he toured the country promoting responsible pet adoptions, pet care, and his favorite food, 9Lives. The company donated millions of dollars in cat food and cash to shelters across the United States. The original Morris died in 1979 but his successors (the current Morris is Number 4) carry on his legend. His picture still hangs on the wall of the Chicago shelter where the greatest cat star of all time was first discovered.

CATTLE CALL

Did you know you can lead a cow upstairs but not down? Here are more quirky bovine facts.

EW, GROSS!
Cows clean their noses with their tongues.

YOU RANG?
Some Japanese farmers have a modern way to let their cows know when it's chow time: pagers. They hang one around each cow's neck. At dinnertime, the beeper goes off and the cows head for the trough.

BEST-DRESSED COWS
British farmers dress their cows in colorfully striped leggings, but not because they want them to be fashionable. It's so drivers can see the cows more easily at night.

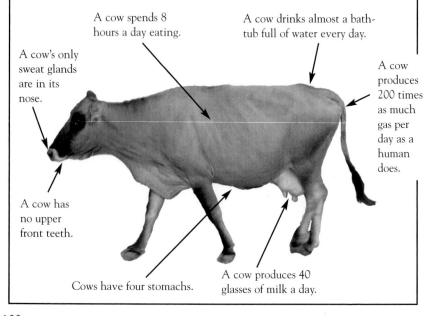

A cow spends 8 hours a day eating.

A cow drinks almost a bathtub full of water every day.

A cow's only sweat glands are in its nose.

A cow produces 200 times as much gas per day as a human does.

A cow has no upper front teeth.

Cows have four stomachs.

A cow produces 40 glasses of milk a day.

SOME PIG!

It's official: Pigs are the smartest animals on the farm.

GAME BOYS

Pigs do tricks, respond to verbal commands, and even play computer games. In one study some porkers used their snouts to move the joystick to shoot at targets and had a hit rate of 80 percent.

NO SWEAT

Did you ever hear the phrase "sweat like a pig"? Guess what? Pigs can't sweat! They don't have sweat glands.

MR. PIG HOGS IT ALL!

A pet porker named Mr. Pig and a dog named Calamity Jane inherited $600,000 when their owner, Margo Lamp, died in 1990. When the dog died, Mr. Pig became the sole inheritor. (Did he keep the money in his piggy bank?)

POODLE DOO

Poodles are smart, strong, fast, and loyal.
So, what's with that wacky hairdo?

Originally, the poodle cut had a practical purpose. The fur was kept thick around the joints and organs for protection in cold water. The rest of its coat was shorn to keep it from getting caught in the brambles. Then, somewhere around the 1700s, owners went a little nutty. Groomers clipped the dogs in any design their owners requested, such as a family coat of arms or monograms. They even sported tiny mustaches and pointy beards. Often they capped the poodle with a pompadour to match the owner's big puffy wig. Poodles were a natural for the circus—smart and talented—and their exaggerated pom-poms matched the round pom-poms on the clowns' costumes.

TELE-CUBBY. A Beauséjour, Canada, teenager was startled to find a bear in his basement, lounging in front of the fireplace, eating potato chips, and watching TV.

COUCH POTATO. A family in Evesham, England, discovered a ferret on their couch, cheerfully watching their telly.

IT'S A HOOT. An owl in Jiangxi, China, loved TV so much that he built his nest in the rafters of one family's home. The owl slept during the day and watched TV from the kitchen table all night.

APE TV. Gorillas at the Moscow Zoo were getting so bored that televisions were installed in their cages. The zoo director said, "We want them to spend less time picking their noses and more time thinking about life."

SMARTY JONES

At the 2004 Kentucky Derby, a little chestnut colt named Smarty Jones won the hearts of Americans because of his champion spirit and his amazing story.

SOMEDAY FARM

Things started out nicely for Smarty. He was born at Someday Farm in New Hope, Pennsylvania, on February 28, 2001. Smarty's owners, Roy and Pat Chapman, wanted to name the spunky colt after Pat's mother, Mildred McNair (who was also born on February 28). But they didn't think "Mildred" was a very good name for a racehorse…so they gave him Mildred's nickname, "Smarty Jones."

DISASTER STRIKES

Nine months later, the Chapmans' horse trainer and his wife were murdered. The shock was so great to the Chapmans that they decided to sell the farm and most of their horses, including Smarty. But on the day of the sale the little horse hid out in the pasture with his mother, so they kept him.

DISASTER STRIKES AGAIN

The Chapmans sent Smarty to a trainer named John Servis in Philadelphia. But tragedy struck again when Smarty reared up and hit his head on an iron bar in the starting gate and collapsed, unconscious. Smarty hit his head so hard he fractured his skull and shattered his eye socket. John Servis thought Smarty had killed himself. Miraculously Smarty lived, but he nearly lost his left eye.

THE COMEBACK KID

After weeks in the hospital and a month of rest, Smarty Jones went back into training. His jockey was a Canadian named Stewart Elliot. Elliot had won thousands of races but had never ridden in the Kentucky Derby. Some

thought of that as a drawback, but it turned out that the partnership between "Stew" Elliot and Smarty Jones was a good one. Smarty won his first eight races—at eight different distances and at five different tracks.

This little champion was making such a splash on the racing scene that one man told the Chapmans to name their price and he'd pay it. Any amount! The Chapmans nearly sold Smarty for millions, but they decided to hold out to see if he could win the Kentucky Derby. They weren't disappointed.

THE WINNER'S CIRCLE

On May 4, 2004, the undersized Thoroughbred with the dent still showing in his head was first across the finish line at the Kentucky Derby. Less than two weeks later, Smarty Jones won the Preakness Stakes and became the first horse in 27 years to win both races.

RANDOM DOG FACTS

• All dogs are descendants of wolves.

• Dogs sweat through the pads of their feet, not by panting.

• A dog's nose print is like a human fingerprint—no two are alike.

• Nine mail carriers a day are bitten by dogs.

HORSE PUCKY

Here's the inside poop on life in the theater.

A TRUE STORY

In a production of *Camelot* in the 1970s, a horse had to appear on stage every night. To make sure that the horse didn't poop on the stage and embarrass everyone, a veterinarian was hired to put his hand up the horse's butt and pull out any waste before the horse appeared on stage. One night, just before the cue, the veterinarian was doing his job when the horse tightened his muscles and the vet's arm got stuck. The cue came and the horse made his entrance—with a man sticking out of his butt!

BEASTLY EXPRESSIONS

More origins of the crazy phrases you may have heard Grandma say.

NEVER LOOK A GIFT HORSE IN THE MOUTH.

Meaning: When you get a gift, don't question it—just accept it with gratitude.

Story: You can tell the age of a horse by looking at its teeth. Checking his age is sort of like looking for the price tag on a gift—you could be in for a big shock.

I SMELL A RAT!

Meaning: Something is terribly wrong.

Story: In the olden days, rats often lived quietly in the walls of houses. People didn't see them, but when their dogs started whimpering and scratching at the walls for no apparent reason, they would say, "Bowser must have smelled a rat."

THAT'S HOGWASH.

Meaning: That's nonsense.

Story: Hogwash was a limp, watery substance that was fed to pigs. It contained leftover scraps and some flour, but nothing very substantial.

ANOTHER MAD COW

Boolah, boolah! Where's your moolah?

DIAMOND IN THE ROUGH

In 2004 a diamond merchant in India hid a bag full of
1,700 small diamonds in a pile of hay at his home.
Unfortunately, his cow ate the hay…and the bag. Since
cows are sacred in India, it never occurred to him to kill
the cow to get the bag. Instead, he followed the cow
around everywhere, picking one diamond at a time out
of the cow's poop.

ANIMAL NEWS

CAT WINS BIG!

One winter's night in 1996 a man named Gayle McManamon saw his cat, Skipper, playing with his lottery shaker (a simple device that some people use to help them pick their lottery numbers). He noticed that Skipper had picked six numbers: 8, 11, 16, 25, 26, and 42.

So the very next day McManamon bought a lottery ticket with the cat's numbers. And amazingly—you guessed it—he won. How much? $3.72 million!

BOOK HOUND

Read all about it.

Wofford, a golden retriever from Norfolk, Virginia, likes to fetch, all right—but not sticks or balls. Wofford is a book hound. He *loves* books. Even as a young pup, Wofford liked to take books to bed with him. He often greets guests at the door by offering them a book. One day Wofford got out of the yard and slipped into the public library. He picked up a children's book and waited in line to check it out. The librarian took the book and tried to offer Wofford a  chew toy instead, but Wofford would have none of it. He headed right back to the stacks and got himself another book.

SPIRIT GUIDES

Many cultures believe that an animal's spirit enters into a person when they are born. Which animal are you?

CAT
Serene

You are extremely independent—no one can tell you what to do. But you can be lovable and playful when you want to be. Above all you are serene, graceful, and love to relax.

BEAR
Patient

You are a patient and wise friend. You love your family but you are just as happy being alone. You may enjoy fishing, hiking, and wrestling with your friends.

DOG
Loyal

You are a loving, fun, and loyal pal. You are eager to help and are always the first to volunteer. You are protective—you can smell trouble coming from a mile away.

DOLPHIN
Cheerful

You are friendly, outgoing, and trustworthy. You know how to find the balance between work and play. You love to talk and you might even like to write or sing.

EAGLE
Alert

You are courageous, observant, and thoughtful. If you are missing, all anyone needs to do is look up—you're probably in a tree watching the world.

ELEPHANT
Compassionate

You are strong and compassionate. You see every moment as an opportunity to learn and you never forget. You love being with your family and friends.

GIRAFFE
Aware

You are intuitive and can see far into the future. You aren't afraid to take risks because you are able to see your dreams come true.

HIPPOPOTAMUS
Protective
You are a gentle soul. Yet when it comes to your home and family you are fiercely protective. You are very inventive and know how to have a good time.

HORSE
Faithful
You are a faithful and wise friend. You find creative solutions to life's problems. You love to travel—especially with a group.

LION
Proud
You are the center of attention—you can't help it. You love playing, working, or just hanging with your family and friends. You know how to chill.

MONKEY
Imaginative
You are energetic, imaginative, and creative. You have a knack for inventing and love to play practical jokes on your family and friends.

PIG
Honorable

You are truthful and honorable—you look out for the little guy. You are smart enough to know that the simple pleasures in life are the best.

RABBIT
Creative

You are creative and intelligent. Being quick thinking, you are an excellent problem solver. You enjoy life— "No Fear" is your motto.

SNAKE
Charming

You are a creative and ambitious leader. Charm is your middle name. Your friends think you are mysterious because you love illusions and have a talent for magic.

TIGER
Powerful

Energetic and powerful, you know what you want and you get it. You are also mischievous and love a good surprise.

VIP'S VIPS
(VERY IMPORTANT PEOPLE'S VERY IMPORTANT PETS)

President Teddy Roosevelt's family had quite a menagerie, including a lion, a hyena, a coyote, five bears, a badger, two parrots, a zebra, a raccoon, an owl, cats, dogs, horses, guinea pigs, and a snake named Emily Spinach. Their pet pony, Algonquin, made a number of secret trips up the White House elevator to visit young Archibald Roosevelt when he was ill.

Sir Isaac Newton, the British physicist from the 1600s, considered one of the most influential scientists of all time, was a cat owner. In addition to discovering gravity, he also invented the cat door.

Walt Disney owned a pet mouse named Mortimer, which was the inspiration for the famous cartoon mouse. His wife Lillian didn't like the name, so he changed it to Mickey Mouse.

MEET PORKCHOP

The Keekorok Lodge in Kenya has an unusual "guard dog" who gallops out to greet the guests. She's a warthog named Porkchop. Porkchop was only two weeks old when she was found stuck in some bushes in the Masai Mara Game Reserve. The lodge owners adopted her and now this little warthog trots around the grounds, pays visits to sunbathers by the pool, and is even up for a game of fetch. However, one roar from hippos in the nearby pond and Porkchop's tail stands straight up and she runs for the nearest place to hide, which could be behind your legs or in your lap!

SNORKEL MASTERS

Did you know that elephants can snorkel? They can walk along the bottom of a river with just the tip of their trunks sticking out for air. They have even been seen snorkeling far out at sea. Some scientists think elephants may have evolved from water creatures because of their snorkeling ability.

DID YOU KNOW?

- Elephants' eyes are only slightly larger than humans'.
- The average elephant weighs less than a blue whale's tongue.
- There are 40,000 muscles in an elephant's trunk.
- Elephants can hear the footsteps of a mouse.
- Elephants cry when a loved one dies.

THEY NEVER FORGET

CASE #1. When a female elephant named Kura was brought to the Shambala Preserve in California, the keepers worried that she wouldn't get along with Timbo, a bull elephant who already lived there. But the moment they saw each other, the two elephants wrapped their trunks together like old friends. It turned out that they had been shipped from Africa on the same freighter more than 40 years earlier.

CASE #2. An elephant in a game park in Kenya had a badly injured foot but wouldn't let anyone get near him to treat it. Finally the vets sent for the elephant's old trainer. He hadn't seen the elephant for 15 years, but the minute he called the elephant by name, it lay down and held up the hurt foot so the vets could take care of it.

THE ELEPHANT
AND THE COWBOY

ORPHAN AMY MEETS BOB

When Amy the elephant first met Bob the cowboy, she was just a baby. She was also an orphan—one of five that had been brought to the United States from Africa by a man who rented stalls at Bob's T-Cross Ranch in Pueblo, Colorado. The man's plan was to sell the orphaned elephants to zoos or circuses. But Amy was sickly and undersized and nobody wanted her... except Bob.

RANCH HAND

Bob Norris saw something special in the tiny elephant,

and he decided to adopt her. The T-Cross Ranch was a working ranch, so Bob put Amy to work, too. He taught her how to lead a horse, separate a single cow from the herd, and feed the goats. When she wasn't working, he taught Amy how to play the piano and the harmonica. She also played with giant beach balls and stuffed animals. Bob took her to the local schools to teach children about elephants. Amy even had her favorite restaurants. She'd wait patiently in the back of the truck while Bob would run in to El Chorros and get her favorite food: sticky buns.

AMY JOINS THE CIRCUS

By the time she was seven, Amy had become too big to live on the ranch. So Bob got her a job with the Big Apple Circus. Amy loved the circus and the circus loved her. But Bob missed Amy more than he'd ever imagined he would. A year later Bob and his wife flew to New York to see Amy perform. They sat in the front row. Bob had brought Amy's favorite sticky buns from El Chorros. He was very nervous: would Amy even know who he was anymore?

AMY AND BOB, TOGETHER AGAIN

The lights came on and the clowns and performers ran into the ring. Finally came the star of the show: Amy. She began her act—and suddenly stopped. Her trunk went up and she sniffed the air. She rumbled and trumpeted. The crowd froze.

What was Amy doing? Suddenly she ran straight to Bob, dropped to her knees, and laid her head in his lap. She touched the tip of her trunk under his chin and all over his face. She made the chirruping sound she always made when she was happy. Bob wrapped his arms around Amy and cried, "She remembers me!"

HOMEWARD BOUND

In his book The Parrot's Lament, *author Eugene Linden tells the story of a remarkable leopard named Harriet.*

As a cub, Harriet had been rescued and taken into the home of a conservationist named Billy Arjun Singh. He raised Harriet to adulthood, then returned her to the forest preserve across the river in northern India where she was born. Harriet's return to the wild was successful and she soon gave birth to two cubs of her own. Everything was fine until the flood season came. As the water rose and filled her den, Harriet quickly had to find a safe place for her cubs.

Where'd she go? Home. One by one, she carried her cubs across the rising river to Billy Singh's house. The leopards stayed in Singh's kitchen until the floodwaters receded. Then she was ready to return to the preserve. She tried to carry the cubs across the river, but the current was too strong. Thinking quickly, Harriet took the cubs to Singh's boat, where she had ridden many times, and dropped her children inside. Then she climbed into the boat and patiently waited until Singh ferried her and her family safely across the raging river, back to her den.

"These amazing true stories confirm what many of us have always suspected—that animals would make better humans than most humans would."
—CARL HIAASEN

THE
Parrot's LAMENT

AND OTHER TRUE TALES OF
ANIMAL INTRIGUE,
INTELLIGENCE, AND INGENUITY

EUGENE LINDEN

YO, DUDE!

How do animals say hello?

HIPPOS are the only animals that can communicate above *and* below the water.

KANGAROO RATS talk by stamping their feet.

PRAIRIE DOGS have one of the most sophisticated animal languages known to science, with more than 100 "words."

MALE GIRAFFES press their necks together to practice their fighting skills.

EXPOSED!

Hold on to your pants.
It's a jungle out there!

Raja was a 14-year-old orangutan who lived at an ape
sanctuary on the Pacific island of Borneo. One day
Raja surprised a French tourist by grabbing him, stripping
off his shirt, pants, and underwear, and then running off
into the forest. The startled Frenchman was left standing
alone on the trail…naked.

YIKES, STRIPES!

*What's black and white and runs all over...Africa?
Answer: the zebra—one of Africa's strangest
creatures. Zebras live in the savannas of
central Africa, and they're closely
related to the horse.*

It's official: Zebras are white with black stripes, not the other way around. So why are they striped? Experts say it's to confuse predators—from lions to tiny tsetse flies—who can't tell where one zebra begins and the other ends. Zebras are instinctively attracted to anything with black-and-white stripes. Even if the stripes are painted on a wall, a zebra will go stand next to them!

Although zebras can be ridden, they can never be domesticated like horses can. Humans have tried for 200 years to get zebras to act like horses, but the zebras refuse to cooperate—they are just too wild and unpredictable to be trained.

DID YOU KNOW?

• No two zebra stripe patterns are alike.

• A zebra crossed with a horse is a *zorse*. A zebra crossed with a donkey is a *zonkey*.

• A zebra's night vision is as good as an owl's.

• Zebras smile. They greet each other with a bared-teeth grimace that helps prevent aggression.

• Zebras travel in herds of as many as 10,000.

• Although most zebras are white with black stripes, a few are actually black with white stripes.

WHAT A BABY!

BABY HARP SEALS are born with totally white fur. The fur provides camouflage on snow and ice. It changes to waterproof, dark brown fur as they grow older.

NEWBORN DUCK-BILLED PLATYPUSES have teeth that help them break out of their eggs. The teeth disappear as they get older.

NEWBORN ARMADILLOS have soft shells, like human fingernails. A natural process called *ossification* causes their shells to harden into bone.

BAT BABIES have no hair when they're born. To keep the babies warm, all of the mother bats and babies huddle together in a bat nursery.

NEWBORN SKUNKS are born hairless with striped black-and-white skin. Their eyes and ears are closed, but careful—they can still spray!

BABY BUFFALO are born without horns or a hump—they start to form when the baby is two months old.

NEWBORN BUSH BABIES are just two inches long and weigh only ½ ounce (about the weight of a tablespoon of water). Bush babies can grow up to be eight inches long—but they will always sound like cry-babies. (That's why they're called bush *babies*.)

POLAR PLUS

WALRUSES use their tusks like canes to walk on land.

The male walrus with the longest tusks usually becomes the leader.

Walruses don't hunt for food with their tusks, but they do use their whiskers, which can sense the movement of fish.

CARIBOU can sleep in water.

SEALS can hold their breath for more than an hour and dive down nearly a mile in the ocean.

Ever seen a seal scoot across the ground? That scooting motion is known as *galluphing*.

AN ARCTIC FOX'S fur can keep it warm and toasty at 100 degrees below zero. At that temperature, you would freeze to death in less than five minutes.

Arctic fox dens are used for centuries, by many generations of foxes. Over the years they become so big that they can have more than 100 entrances.

WOLF TALK

According to scientists, wolves have a unique way of communicating. Here's how it works.

BARK: Warning! Danger!

BARED TEETH: Don't come any closer.

WHIMPER: Mother does this to calm the pups.

HEAD AND EARS UP HIGH: I'm the boss.

EARS BACK AND SQUINT: I'm afraid.

DANCE AND BOW: Want to play?

HIGH WHINE OR SQUEAKING SOUND: Puppies, come here!

WAG JUST THE TIP OF THE TAIL: I'm about to attack.

TAIL BETWEEN LEGS: You're the boss.

WOLF HOWL: Everyone! Bring the pack together!

DID YOU KNOW?

- A wolf's pawprint can be bigger than a human hand.
- A wolf's tail hangs, while a dog's tail tends to stick up.
- A dog's ears are pointed; a wolf's are rounded.
- Every wolf pack has a leader. He's called the alpha male.

GOING BATTY

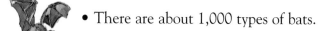

- There are about 1,000 types of bats.

- Disc-winged bats of South America have sticky patches on their wings and feet, which allow them to live inside banana leaves.

- Bats are the only mammal that can truly fly.

- Generally, bats will turn left when coming out of a cave.

- The scientific name for bat is *Chiroptera*, which is Greek for "hand-wing."

- Vampire bats adopt orphans.

- A bat's leg bones are too thin to walk on.

- Woolly bats of West Africa live in the large webs of colonial spiders.

- A bat can eat as many as 1,200 insects in an hour.

- Texas has more bats than any other state. Bracken Cave alone is home to 20 million Mexican free-tailed bats.

LIFE ON EASY CREEK

In 2004 someone pulled a heist at the Lucky Dollar Casino in Greensburg, Louisiana, and stole $75,000. Sheriff's deputies tracked down the crooks but couldn't find the stolen money. Then a lawyer hoping to make a deal for one of the crooks called prosecutors and revealed that the money had been tossed into a nearby creek.

Officers raced to the creek and found one of the money bags floating in the brush and another leaning against a beaver dam.

When they drained the pond, they found the third bag…empty. Apparently a pair of beavers had found it first, and had woven thousands of soggy bills into the walls of their dam. When cops broke open the dam to retrieve the bills, they couldn't believe their eyes—the interior looked like it had been decorated with money wallpaper!

WRONG!

Some animal names just don't fit.

FLYING FOXES aren't foxes. They're bats. They live in Australia and they're huge. In fact, with a wingspan of up to six feet, they're the largest bats in the world! And, unlike foxes, they eat only fruit.

MOUNTAIN BEAVERS aren't beavers and they don't live in the mountains. They are muskratlike rodents that live mostly in the coastal forests of the Pacific Northwest. With their short, stubby bodies and no tail, they look like groundhogs.

CRABEATER SEALS do *not* eat crabs! They eat krill, a tiny shrimplike animal in the icy waters around Antarctica. They were misnamed in 1837 by the French explorer Jules Dumont d'Urville.

PRAIRIE DOGS are not dogs—they're rodents. They live in large underground colonies called townships. However, they do have a sharp bark that sounds like a dog's.

PICK THE WEIRDEST NOSE

STAR-NOSED MOLES

have the most complex noses in the animal kingdom. Their noses have tentacles, which they use to detect insect prey. No other nose is as sensitive to the touch (or as weird looking) as the star-nosed mole's.

BATS can detect the warmth of an animal from six inches away using their "nose-leaf."

The male **PROBOSCIS MONKEY** has a really big nose—sometimes it's so big the monkey has to hold it aside with one hand so it can eat! The purpose of giant schnoz is unclear, but scientists think it may help the monkeys stay cool in the humid swamps of southeast Asia.

ANIMAL NEWS
INVASION OF THE ARMADILLOS

A stranger is taking over our farms, forests, and neighborhoods! An invader from Central America, protected by bands of sturdy

body armor, is expanding its range across the United States 10 times faster than other mammals. As many as 50 million of these invaders are already here.

Who is this creature? It's the nine-banded armadillo. This rabbit-sized mammal prospers in areas where others fail. Why? Because the armadillo not only has lots of babies but also chooses when to have them. The pregnant female can delay birth for up to two years until she finds a safe place to raise her kids. (The armadillo is the only mammal that always has four identical girls or boys.) Plus, an armadillo can live up to 20 years, which means that just a few armadillos can quickly take over a new area.

Can anything stop the armadillo from overrunning North America? Yes. Cold. Armadillos don't like it. They can't survive temperatures below freezing. So those of you in Alaska, Montana, Minnesota, and all of those icy northern states can relax. The armadillo invasion won't be coming your way.

ARMOR-DILLOS

• There are 20 species of armadillo, but the nine-banded armadillo is the only one that lives in North America. The other 19 live in South America.

• Startle an armadillo and it will jump three to four feet straight up in the air!

• Armadillos walk on their tiptoes.

• The giant armadillo can weigh over 120 pounds and be up to five feet long.

• Armadillos eat six *billion* pounds of bugs in the U.S. every year!

• An armadillo without its shell looks like a hairless rabbit.

WILD AND WOOLLY FACT

Armadillos are the submarines of the animal world. Their heavy shells make them sink, so they can walk along the bottom of a river. If they want to float, they gulp air into their intestines and float on the surface like a balloon.

BRIGHT IDEAS

Some examples of how humans take care of troubled animals.

PROBLEM: Too many squirrels from a rare colony in England were being killed while crossing a busy highway.

SOLUTION: The authorities built rope bridges to help the squirrels get safely to the other side of the road.

PROBLEM: Orphaned baby kangaroos, or *joeys*, can't survive for long outside their mother's pouch.

SOLUTION: Australians make cotton "joey bags" that resemble kangaroo pouches and hang them from baby bouncer frames. The orphan joey stays inside until it grows fur and can survive on its own.

PROBLEM: During a fire, pets are far more sensitive to the effects of smoke than humans are.

SOLUTION: A Florida fire department got some specially sized oxygen masks from a local vet. Now cats, dogs, and even hamsters suffering from smoke inhalation can be given a breath of life-saving air.

GHOST PETS

GHOST RIDERS IN THE SKY

In the suburbs of Chicago there is a horseriding trail that crosses a very busy street. Over its long history, many riders and horses have been killed trying to cross the street. A traffic light was finally placed there, which made it much safer. But now, when it's night or near dusk, some drivers have reported seeing what appears to be a horse and rider trying to cross the street. The motorists slow down, trying to get a better view, and suddenly the ghostly duo just disappears into thin air. Other ghostly steeds have been seen: one throwing his rider from the saddle and another being dragged sideways down the highway.

WAKE UP, WALTER!

One day, Walter Manuel of Los Angeles dreamed that his dog Lady was barking frantically trying to wake him. Lady had died just three weeks earlier, but the dream seemed so real that he couldn't help rushing to the bedroom window to see if anything was wrong. He was shocked to see his two-year-old son fall into the swimming pool. Thanks to Lady's ghost, Manuel was able to save his little boy.

WATER DOGS

They're wet and wild (and woolly).

SCUBA-DOO

Shadow is a half golden, half Labrador retriever from Boynton Beach, Florida, who loves to spend time not just *in* the water—but *under* the water. Shadow is a scuba diver. Using special dive gear designed by her owner, Dwane Folsom, Shadow can stay underwater for an hour. Her favorite dive buddy, other than Dwane, is a moray eel.

X-TREME MASTER

Part-X is running out of extreme sports to try. This Jack Russell terrier from Cornwall, England, has mastered surfing, cliff-jumping, rappelling, and sea kayaking. Now he's learning to water ski in his own custom-made life jacket. Part-X got the bug for extreme sports in 2000 when he jumped on his owner's surf board and rode his first wave. "Whenever we go near moving water Part-X gets really, really excited," says owner J.P. Eatock. "He even tries to woof and bite the wave as we surf." Next: crossing the Irish Sea by kayak and a tandem sky dive with J.P.

I'M BACK!

Three stories about pets that found their way home.

AUSTRALIAN WALKABOUT. In October 1973 a collie named Whisky became separated from his master while vacationing in Darwin in northern Australia. Nine months later, Whisky had found his way home. The collie had traveled an amazing 1,802 miles across Australia— and through the rugged Outback—to reach the southern city of Melbourne…and his master's home.

DODGING BULLETS. When Private James Brown went to France to fight in World War I, he left his Irish terrier, Prince, at home in England. A month later, on September 27, 1914, his wife wrote to him with the sad news that Prince was missing. The letter didn't upset Private Brown—his devoted dog had already joined him in the trenches. Prince had somehow crossed the English Channel (probably as a stowaway on a boat) and walked another 60 miles through battlefields to find his best friend in Armentières, France. That was a trip of 200 miles.

MARATHON CAT. A tabby cat named McCavity didn't like his new home in Cumbernauld, Scotland, even though his family was with him. One day he just up and left. Three weeks and 497 miles later, McCavity was found meowing at the front door of his old home in Truro, England. McCavity had walked 25 miles a day for 21 days—that's almost a marathon a day.

DREAMING OF CATS

According to some dream experts...

- *If you dream of a* tortoise-shell cat, *you'll be* lucky in love.

- *If you dream of a* ginger (orange) cat, *you'll be* lucky in money and business.

- *If you dream of a* tabby cat, *you'll be* lucky at home.

- *If you dream of a* black-and-white cat, *you'll be* lucky with children.

- *If you dream of a* multi-colored cat, *you'll be* lucky with making new friends.

- *If you dream of a* black cat, *you'll be* lucky in all things.

FOND FAREWELLS

They loved their pets so much that when they died...

King Charles IX of France had his greyhound Courte made into hunting gloves.

King Edward VII of England had his terrier Jack's hair made into a bracelet.

Roy Rogers, the singing cowboy movie star of the 1950s, had his horse, Trigger, and his dog, Bullet, stuffed and put on display at the Roy Rogers and Dale Evans Museum in Branson, Missouri.

U   U   U

ANIMAL EPITAPHS

A few funny epitaphs found on tombstones in New York's Hartsdale Canine Cemetery, America's first pet cemetery.

Grumpy
"His sympathetic love and understanding enriched our lives"

Penny
"She never knew she was a rabbit"

Thor Dog
"A cat"

Hoppy
"Our three-legged wonder"

GOTTA GO!

PACHYDERM POTTY

Elephants in Thailand are already taught to paint,
dance, and play musical instruments. What's next?
They're being toilet trained.

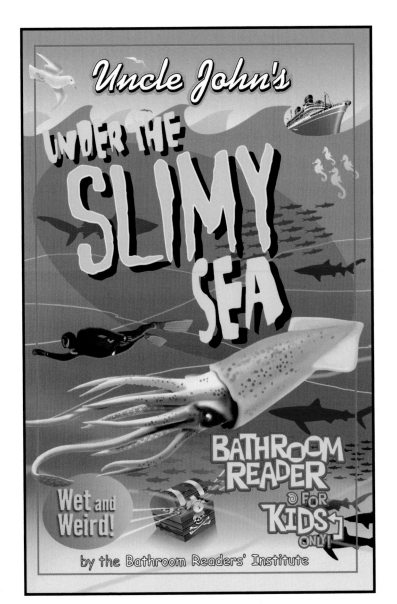

Uncle John's

UNDER THE SLIMY SEA

BATHROOM READER FOR KIDS ONLY!

Wet and Weird!

by the Bathroom Readers' Institute

Notes from an Old Sea Dog

A hoy, Kids!
It's me, Porter the Wonder Dog…again. As a Portuguese Water Dog (that's really what I am), I thought I knew a thing or two about the sea. But it turns out there's more to it than just "it's wet, and you swim in it." Other things swim in it, too. There's sharks, lobsters, sharks, krill, sharks, whales, sharks, plankton, sharks, dolphins, and a whole lot of other slimy, finny, and scary creatures. And sharks.

So have fun with Part Two of *Creature Feature*:

Under the Slimy Sea!

(And watch out for sharks.)

MR. BLOBBY

People have always wondered what lurks in the deepest parts of the ocean. Now scientists are beginning to find out—and the results aren't pretty...

Meet Mr. Blobby. He's a *blobfish*. (He's sometimes called a *fathead fish*, too, but why add insult to injury?) He's only one foot in length, and lives 3,000 feet below the surface. This part of the ocean is called the *mesopelagic* zone, also known as the "twilight zone" because very little sunlight reaches it. This guy looks like a blob of Jell-O because that's pretty much what he is. His goopy flesh is just a bit lighter than water, so he doesn't need to use any muscles or oxygen to keep from sinking to the bottom. Like many creatures that live at this great depth, blobfish are "sit-and-wait" predators—they wait patiently for their dinner to drift within reach of their mouths. Then...*gulp!*

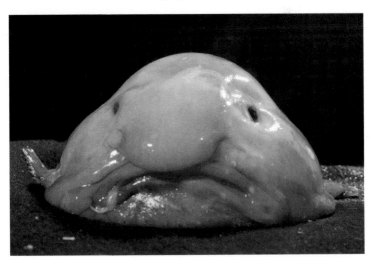

DOLPHIN FACTS

➤ Dolphins are born with mustaches. (So are whales.)

➤ A dolphin can hold its breath for up to eight minutes and dive as deep as 1,000 feet.

➤ Dolphins never take a drink. They absorb all their water from their food.

➤ Dolphins sleep with one eye shut—half of their brain rests; the other half (and the other eye) stays awake.

 Every dolphin has signature whistles, or "names," that it uses to find its family and friends.

 The largest dolphin is the *orca*, or killer whale, which can grow to 31.5 feet long (about 10 meters).

➤ The smallest? It's a tie between Hector's dolphin and the black dolphin. Adults can be as short as four feet long (1.2 meters).

OCEAN ACROBATS

Dolphins are graceful and athletic. They're the stars of aquarium shows the world over, dazzling audiences with soaring flips and dives. But the superstars are the *spinner dolphins*. These mammals got their name from their signature jump: They can leap out of the water and rotate up to seven times, like an ice skater doing an axel jump. Spinners have other great moves, too: tail slaps, fluke dives, nose-outs, and spectacular head-over-tail flips.

Like all dolphins, spinners love to play. One of their favorite games is "make a play-toy." Anything floating in the water—a fishing float, a lump of driftwood—becomes "it." Spinners will play catch with the object, and even wear it on their heads like a hat. They're so much fun to watch that Hawaiians call them "Ambassadors of Aloha."

Dolphin researchers have studied spinners to figure out why they jump and spin, and have come up with a few explanations. Sometimes they spin to get rid of a pesky parasite. Sometimes a spinner wants to signal the rest of the pod exactly where it is (in this case, the spin ends with a loud belly-flop). But the best explanation for why spinners spin is, well, because they can.

IS SAND FISH POOP?

Well, some of it is—particularly on the coral reefs of the Indian and Pacific Oceans. Coral are actually small animals, related to sea anemones, that protect their soft bodies with a limestone covering. Coral gather in colonies that number in the millions. Each new generation of coral builds on the skeleton of the previous one, and over time coral reefs become home to all kinds of sea life. Those limestone skeletons are literally hard as a rock, but that doesn't bother the *bumphead parrotfish.*

Bumpheads love to eat the algae that grow on the coral. Rather than pick it off bit by bit, they use their strong jaws to chomp right through the rock, which they swallow along with the algae. Then they poop it out as fine white sand. On a single reef, bumpheads can crank out a ton of sand every year. Over centuries the sand builds up to make tropical islands. So those beautiful white beaches you see on postcards of tropical paradises are really nothing but a load of fish poop!

GNARLY TEETH

QUESTION:

What's got a hard shell, weighs more than 1,000 pounds, and has a mouthful of truly gnarly "teeth"?

ANSWER:
THE LEATHERBACK TURTLE

Well, maybe not *actually* teeth. What this ocean reptile has is a mouthful of stiff spines that point backwards to help it swallow its favorite food—jellyfish!

MONSTER WAVES

So you want to be a sailor? You may change your mind after you read this.

WALL OF WATER

What's a monster wave? One that rises 80 feet or more above the ocean's surface. Imagine a wall of water ¼ mile wide and as high as a 10-story building bearing down on

you like a freight train. That's a monster wave! Sometimes they're called "freaks" and "rogues." The biggest wave ever measured at sea was 98 feet tall. Most monster waves are caused by hurricanes and other storms. Others happen when waves join great ocean currents like the Gulf Stream. But wherever they come from, they're deadly— monster waves can snap a giant tanker ship in half like a toothpick. Worst of all, it takes hundreds of miles for one to build up to monster size. A ship can be sailing on a clear day far from a storm and still get slammed by a monster wave.

HOOK, LINE, AND SINKER

Q: *What do you call a fish with no eye?*
A: FSH!

Q: *How do you keep a fish from smelling?*
A: Cut off its nose.

Q: *If fish lived on land, which country would they live in?*
A: Finland.

Q: *What did the boy octopus say to the girl octopus?*
A: I want to hold your hand hand hand hand hand hand hand hand.

Q: *Why are fish smarter than mice?*
A: Because they live in schools.

SEA ANIMAL QUIZ #1: WHAT IS THIS MYSTERIOUS GIANT?

IT'S BIG...

...As in the biggest creature that ever lived. In fact, this giant is larger than a brontosaurus and a Tyrannosaurus rex put together.

- Its tongue weighs as much as an elephant.
- Its heart is as big as a car.
- Some of its blood vessels are so wide that a person could swim down them.

REALLY BIG...

The largest one ever measured was 108 feet long and weighed almost 190 *tons*. If you stood one on its tail, it would be as tall as a 10-story building. You'd have to stack up more than 25 elephants to equal its weight.

AND FAST...

It can swim at speeds of up to 48 mph, making it one of the fastest swimmers in the world.

AND HUNGRY...

It spends its summers in the icy waters around Antarctica eating *krill*, tiny shrimp-like crustaceans that live there in huge swarms. A single one of these creatures can eat 40 million krill in a day.

AND LOUD!

Our mystery mammal is the loudest creature ever recorded. A jet plane can reach a volume of 120 decibels. A gunshot might hit 140 decibels. But this monster's call clocks in at 180 decibels and can be heard for thousands of miles underwater.

WHAT IS IT?

ANSWER:

THE BLUE WHALE!

This marvelous creature is also one of the most mysterious. Scientists are just beginning to understand some of its habits, but there's much they still don't know, such as where it breeds, or where it migrates. Sadly, we may never find out because the blue whale has been hunted almost to extinction. Almost half a million were killed in the 19th century for their blubber. Scientists guess that there might be as few as 2,000 left. Because they are so rare, today there is a worldwide ban on hunting the blue whale.

FIERCE GUARDIANS

Swimming in Hawaii? Don't forget your aumakua!

Many Hawaiians believe that guardian spirits protect their family. The guardians, known as *aumakua*, often take the form of a powerful animal, such as the shark. As long as the family takes care of their *aumakua*, the shark will take care of them.

• In the 1930s, a tour boat sank off the island of Molokai. Sharks attacked and everyone was killed...except the captain, who later said he had called his *aumakua*. When the shark appeared, it offered the captain its dorsal fin and pulled the man safely past the other sharks to the shore.

• A man from Maui and his wife were sailing to a neighboring island when a sudden squall capsized the boat and swept them into the rough seas. As they foundered in

the water, the man called out, "If I have any *aumakua* in this ocean, I pray you to carry us to the land." A streak flashed by them and a shark appeared in the water. They grabbed the shark by the tail, and it towed them safely to shore.

conversation with ground control and suddenly they're gone, as if they've flown into a hole in the sky.

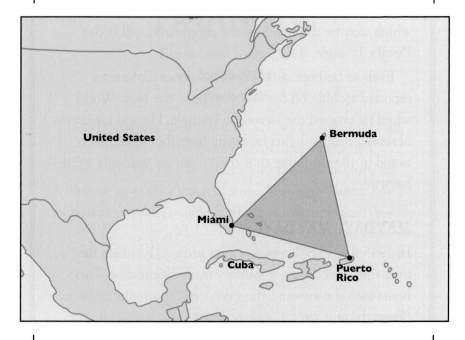

UNSOLVED MYSTERY

What causes compasses to go wild and lights to appear in the sky? Some say that in this area of the ocean is a pocket of magnetic energy that affects electronic gear. Others speak of black holes that send planes and ships into some kind of time warp. Geologist Dr. Richard McIver thought that undersea landslides might cause the release of huge amounts of methane gas which would make the sea look like it's boiling and create clouds of odd-colored light. Some folks whisper about aliens in UFOs abducting the people and planes.

What do *you* think?

FALSE ALARM

Ew. What's that smell?

In December 2006, an alarm went off in the aquarium at the Weymouth Sea Life Center in England. Marine biologist Sarah Leaney raced to the tank to see what was wrong, but found nothing out of order. As she looked at the alarm sensor, a sea turtle floating by ripped off a couple of farts that set the alarm off again. Leaney quickly realized what had happened: The staff had fed the turtle a holiday treat of Brussels sprouts. It seemed that vegetable has the same effect of turtles as it does on people when they eat too much of it—it produces a mighty, stinky wind!

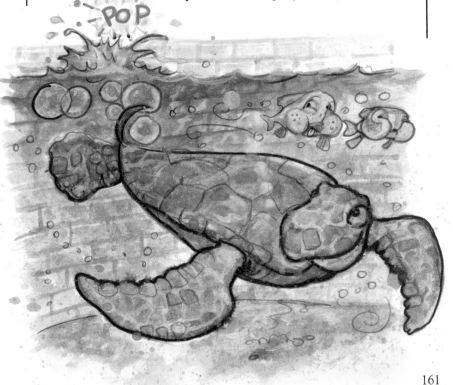

THE WORLD'S SAFEST BEACH? HA!

New Smyrna Beach, Florida, may be the shark bite capital of the world.

According to the International Shark Attack File, two-thirds of all shark attacks in the United States occur in Volusia County, Florida. Most of those take place at New Smyrna Beach, a place once advertised by local businessmen as "the world's safest bathing beach." In August 2001, ten people, most of them surfers, were bitten in as many days. The "world's safest beach" was closed for 10 days while thousands of black-tip sharks cruised by off the coast on their annual migration north. Experts used to think black-tip sharks weren't a threat to people...but not any more!

PREY
(aka "doofuses,
sharkbait")

PREDATORS
(they're
everywhere!)

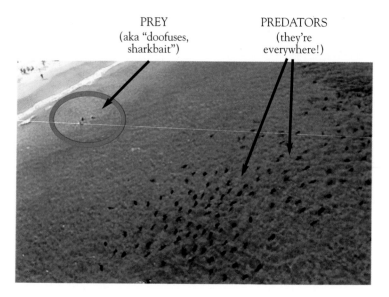

SHARK FACTS

➤ Sharks have no bones. Their skeletons are made of cartilage, the same stuff that's in your ears and your nose.

➤ Sharks are ancient. They were patrolling the oceans more than 300 million years ago—nearly 75 million years before the dinosaurs were around.

➤ Scientists think sharks were the first creatures to have teeth.

➤ A shark can detect a single drop of blood in a million drops (25 gallons) of water.

➤ If it doesn't keep swimming, a shark will sink.

➤ Sharks can sense vibrations in water, and they can detect electrical currents. They use these skills to find their prey.

FISH SALON

If cleaner fish could speak, their
favorite word would be, "Next!"

L ife for a fish is tough. It spends every waking minute trying to eat other fish and avoid being eaten. But there's one class of fish that gets a free pass from the "I'm gonna eat you first" rule: cleaner fish. These tiny fish (mostly *wrasses* and *gobies* the size of minnows) have carved out a special niche for themselves in the sea.

Most fish suffer from parasites—little bugs that latch onto scales and gills like ticks on a dog. But unlike dogs, fish can't scratch. So they line up at cleaning stations set up by cleaner fish in caves or overhangs. The cleaner fish crowd around each "customer" fish and nibble off all of the pests. They even do a teeth cleaning, swimming safely in and out of the gaping jaws of their guests. They work hard, too—researchers on Australia's Great Barrier Reef logged some cleaner fish servicing 2,000 fish a day.

Being a cleaner isn't just a job for fish. There are cleaner shrimp, and even seagulls. But it's a sweet deal for the ones that take on the job: They get an unlimited supply of food (up to 1,200 parasites a day—yum!), and best of all, they don't get eaten by their clients.

DID YOU KNOW...

...the world's only underwater mailbox can be found 32.8 feet below the surface in Susami Bay, Japan? Diver Heinze Pieorkowski put it there on April 23, 1999, but he didn't say why.

FLIPPER

The first dolphin superstar was a female named Mitzi.

One night a stuntman named Ricou Browning was watching the TV show *Lassie* with his kids and thought, "Wouldn't it be great to do a show like this with a boy and a dolphin?" Ricou took his idea to producer Ivan Tors, and the movie *Flipper* was born. A dolphin

named Mitzi was chosen to be the star. Mitzi was smart: She could fetch five things at once, tow a boat with a rope, shake hands, hit the water with her tail, and give someone a ride with her flipper. Her best trick was carrying a boy on her back, which she learned by playing fetch: One day Ricou tossed his nine-year-old son into the water and told Mitzi to retrieve him. The dolphin put her fin under the boy's arm and brought him right back.

The movie *Flipper* came out in 1963, and was a huge success. Another movie was made, followed by a TV series. By then Mitzi had retired. She was replaced by another female dolphin named Suzy, who played Flipper from 1964 to 1967.

SEA DOGS

Aye, matey, it's those two-legged
scourges of the sea—pirates.

BLACKBEARD. The most feared pirate of them all was Blackbeard, a true Pirate of the Caribbean. Blackbeard (his real name was Edward Teach) went into battle with six pistols strapped across his chest and smoking fuses woven into his wild hair and beard. This merciless villain was known to shoot his own crew because, he said, "If I don't shoot one every now and again, they'll forget who I am." When he discovered that the woman he loved had given a ring to another sailor, he attacked her boyfriend's ship and mailed the man's severed hand—with the ring still on it—to the lady. He terrorized the Caribbean and the Atlantic off the Carolina coast from 1716 to 1718 in his ship, *Queen Anne's Revenge.* His final battle was against the *Pearl,* a British ship led by pirate hunter Robert Maynard. Trapped in a shallow bay, Blackbeard fought like a madman to the end. Maynard wrote in his report that Blackbeard was stabbed 20 times and shot five times before he finally fell. They cut off the pirate's head and hung it from the

bowsprit as a warning to all other pirate wannabes. But Blackbeard had the last word. Legend has it that when his headless body was thrown overboard, it swam around the *Pearl* five times…looking for its head.

BARTHOLOMEW ROBERTS. "Black Bart" Roberts came to piracy late (he was 37), but he was the most successful pirate of all time. Born in Wales, he roamed the seas from Brazil to Africa to Newfoundland, capturing and looting more than 400 ships during his career. He designed his own pirate flag, which had a giant figure of himself, cutlass in hand, standing on two skulls. Roberts' life of crime came to an end when he was killed by a hail of gunfire in a battle off the coast of West Africa in 1722.

BLACK CAESAR. Henri "Black" Caesar was born a slave in Haiti in 1765. He worked in a sawmill, where he was mistreated by a white overseer. In 1791 Haitian slaves revolted against their masters and Caesar joined the fight, starting first by executing his overseer with a crosscut saw. When peace came in 1804, he turned to piracy and quickly became feared across the Caribbean for his ferocity in battle and his skill as a sailor. He later moved his base to the west coast of Florida, and is supposed to have buried millions in loot on Sanibel Island. Unlike most pirates of his day, Black Caesar didn't end his life at the end of a rope. In fact, no one knows what became of him. He just vanished.

MADAME CHING

One of the greatest pirates of all time was...a woman!

Madame Ching terrorized the waters off the coast of China in the early years of the 19th century. At the height of her power, she commanded a fleet of 1,800 ships and 70,000 men. But she didn't get to the top by being nice. If one of her pirates broke her rules, she had his head lopped off.

Although Madame Ching terrorized the Chinese navy for years, she was able to do what few pirates ever accomplished: die of old age. In exchange for giving up piracy, the Chinese Navy granted her a pardon in 1810. Madame Ching was even allowed to keep all of her stolen treasure. She used it to open up a gambling house, which she ran for the rest of her life.

YO HO HO!

Avast, ye landlubbers! If ye wanna be a pirate, get your sea legs and take this quiz afore ye set sail.

1. When a pirate is "tipping the blackspot," he is:

a) Making a death threat.

b) Swabbing a dirty deck.

c) Removing his eye patch.

d) Asking for the pepper.

2. What is a "poop deck"?

a) The place where seagulls like to poop on a ship.

b) The deck above the captain's quarters at the stern (rear) of the ship.

c) Where pirates go to the bathroom, also known as the "head."

d) A deck of cards with all the aces missing.

3. When a pirate says "shiver me timbers," he's saying:

a) It's cold out here, matey!

b) The wind's a-blowing and the ship's a creaking.

c) Whoa…what the heck was that?

d) He's singing a work song. ("Shiver me timbers, hoist them sails; let's get this bucket out of the gale.")

4. What are "long clothes"?

a) Rough weather gear pirates wore when sailing through hurricanes.

b) The dresses female pirates wore.

c) Baggy pants and loose jackets that only landlubbers wore.

d) A type of sail used when running down wind.

5. What is a *Yellow Jack*?

a) Pirate slang for a yellow jacket.

b) The name of a legendary sea monster known to have sunken many a ship to "Davy Jones' locker."

c) A warning flag. When a Yellow Jack is flown, it means there's a contagious illness (like the plague) on board.

d) The name of a famous merman.

6. When a pirate *takes a caulk,* he's:

a) Taking a nap on deck.

b) Brushing his teeth.

c) Going to the bathroom.

d) Shipwrecked on a deserted island.

ANSWERS:

1. a) When a pirate delivers a death threat, he slips his victim a piece of paper with a black smudge on one side.

2. b) A poop deck is the highest deck on a sailing ship.

3. c) He's saying he's as surprised as if his ship had just run aground (which would make the masts shiver).

4. c) Pirates couldn't risk wearing anything loose fitting

5. c) Merchant ships often flew a Yellow Jack to keep pirate ships from attacking them.

that might get in their way while climbing the masts to trim the sails in foul weather.

6. a) A "caulk" of black tar and rope was stuffed between the planks on a ship's deck to keep water from leaking in. When pirates slept on deck, they'd often wake up with black lines across their faces from the caulk.

171

THE "DEEP" WOODS

Welcome to the kelp forest, where seaweed hundreds of feet high is home to all kinds of sea creatures.

This forest isn't made of trees—it's made of a type of seaweed called *giant kelp*. Kelp forests flourish in cool offshore waters all around the world. Unlike trees, kelp doesn't put down roots in the sand; it latches onto rocks with its finger-like growths called *holdfasts*. And once it does, look out! Kelp can grow 300 feet in a year. That's almost a foot a day! Why does it grow so fast? Because like all plants, kelp need sunlight to live, and the sunlight is up at the surface. As soon as the stipe (stalk) of the kelp plant reaches the ocean surface, its leaves (called *blades*) spread out in a vast canopy, much like the Amazon rain forest, only underwater. That canopy provides a protected shelter for fish, lobsters, crabs, clams, rays, and seals, as well as tons of food for them to eat. Every winter, ocean storms rip many of the kelp plants off the rocks and cast them on shore, destroying the forest. And every spring a new forest grows up to replace the old one.

DOWN, DOWN, WA-A-A-Y DOWN...

How low can you go in the ocean?
Here's a guide to the ocean zones.

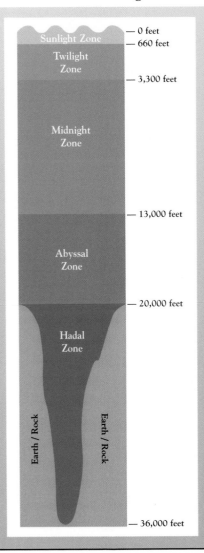

Sunlight Zone
— 0 feet
— 660 feet

Twilight Zone
— 3,300 feet

Midnight Zone

— 13,000 feet

Abyssal Zone

— 20,000 feet

Hadal Zone

Earth / Rock   Earth / Rock

— 36,000 feet

SUNLIGHT ZONE
0–660 feet deep

Also called the *euphotic* zone, this is the top layer of the ocean, and home to 90% of life in the sea. Why? The sun. Its light and warmth make this a great place for plants to grow, and for the fish and mammals that eat them. But with all that sunlight there's no place to hide, so many species use *countershading* to disguise themselves—they're often dark on top and light on their bellies. From above, they blend with the dark water below; from below, they blend with the bright water above.

THE TWILIGHT ZONE 660–3,300 *feet deep*

Also called the *dysphotic* zone, it's too dim for plants to grow. How do creatures down here survive? By feeding on each other. Inhabitants of this zone have to be able to handle cold temperatures and intense water pressure. Some fish have extra-big eyes to help them see, while others make their own light with special organs in their bodies called *photophores*. Scientists call that process *bioluminescence*. Many twilight zone inhabitants have thin bodies to make it harder for predators to see them. Fish in this zone don't chase their food; they either stalk it…or wait for it.

THE MIDNIGHT ZONE 3,300–13,000 *feet deep*

Also called the *aphotic* zone, this is the first ocean layer where there's no light at all. Here the water is always just above freezing and pitch black. The water pressure can be as great as two tons per square inch! Only 1% of sea life, including the mysterious giant squid, lives in this zone, but some surface animals, such as the sperm whale, can dive down to these depths to hunt them.

THE ABYSSAL ZONE 13,000–20,000 *feet deep*

The *abyssal* zone is the *truly* deep sea, but unlike the desert-like quality of the midnight zone, there's lots of life here. Covering 85% of the ocean floor, this is the single largest habitat on Earth. Most of the deep is a great plain covered in thick goopy mud called *sediment*. The burrowing *sea pig* and other odd creatures of the deep get their food from eating the muck.

THE HADAL ZONE 20,000–36,000 *feet deep*

For most of the ocean, the abyssal zone is as low as you can go. But there are huge canyons in the ocean floor that go far deeper. This is the *Hadal* zone, named for Hades, the ancient Greek god of the Underworld. These great underwater gorges are miles below the surface, and for years scientists believed nothing could survive the crushing water pressure. Then, in 1960, explorers Jacques Piccard and Don Walsh took a specially built submarine named the *Trieste* to the bottom of the deepest underwater canyon, the Mariana Trench near the Philippines. They dropped to a depth of 35,800 feet—a feat no one has ever matched. To their amazement, they spotted some shrimp-like creatures and flatfish swimming at the bottom of the world.

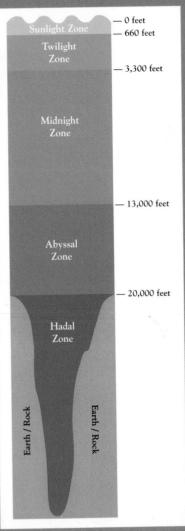

Sunlight Zone — 0 feet
— 660 feet

Twilight Zone
— 3,300 feet

Midnight Zone

— 13,000 feet

Abyssal Zone

— 20,000 feet

Hadal Zone

Earth / Rock   Earth / Rock

DUMBO

This deep sea octopus swims with its "ears."

"Dumbo" is an octopus that lives 1,000 feet down in the ocean. Until BBC film crews filmed it while making the documentary *The Blue Planet*, no one had ever seen an octopus like it before. Those big flaps behind its eyes look like ears, but they're actually fins. *Grimpoteuthis* (Dumbo's scientific name) swims by pushing water through its funnel, flapping its webbed arms, or paddling with its finny "ears." Or it can use all three methods at the same time. "Dumbo" is less than 5 inches long and likes to swim just above the seafloor, where it can dart down and snag snails and worms. There are actually 14 different types of "Dumbo" octopuses, but other than that we don't know much about them at all.

NO BRAIN?
NO PROBLEM

They don't have brains, hearts, or even bones—
they just drift silently and carry a big sting!

Jellyfish aren't fish. They're invertebrate (boneless) animals related to coral and anemones, and have lived in the seas for over 650 million years. There are more than 2,000 species of them: Some are just an inch wide while others, such as the *Nomura*, have a "bell" (body)

larger than a beach umbrella and weigh more than 450 pounds! The monster of all jellyfish is the *Arctic lion's mane*: One was found with a bell more than seven feet wide and tentacles 120 feet long. What the jelly lacks in body parts it makes up for with its sting. Jellyfish have a net of stinging tentacles that paralyze and kill their prey quickly. That keeps a jelly's fragile body from getting torn apart in a struggle.

SPOOK(Y) FISH!

These bug-eyes have a flashlight in their butt!

Discovered by a BBC documentary crew in 1993, *winteria* are known more commonly as *barreleyes* or *spookfish* because of their huge eyes. Spookfish live far below the sunlight zone at depths of up to 6,500 feet, which is why they developed such sensitive eyes. They're tiny, only about six inches long, which is probably why no one found them before. But what's *really* bizarre about this fish is that it has a light organ in its rectum that shines a light out behind it.

Why would a spookfish have the biological equivalent of a flashlight in its butt? Observation revealed that these fish hang vertically in the water, with their big eyes staring up for any prey swimming above them. Scientists think the spookfish probably uses the light shining out of its butt as a form of *counter-illumination* to help it blend in with the dim light coming down from the surface, making the spookfish virtually invisible to its prey.

SURFIN' SNAILS

They ride the surf to catch their dinner!

The *plough snail* from South Africa likes to eat dead things that have been washed up onto the beach. When this super-sensitive snail detects the chemical traces of something good and dead in the water, it makes a beeline for the carcass—but not by leaving a slime trail across the sand like any other snail. No, this snail surfs! It uses its large fleshy foot like a surfboard to ride the waves right to its food. Its unique way of getting up and down the beach makes the plough snail the fastest snail in the world.

AND THE WINNER IS...

Meet some superlative members of the fish family.

THE BIGGEST

The largest **whale shark** ever seen was 65 feet long. That's about 1½ times longer than a school bus.

THE SMALLEST

A tiny **carp** from Sumatra is less than a ⅓ of an inch long. Its name is *Paedocypris progenitica*. (Say that 10 times really fast!)

THE FASTEST

The **sailfish** has been clocked swimming at 67 miles per hour.

THE SLOWEST

The **sea horse** pokes along at $\frac{1}{100}$th of a mile per hour. At that rate, it would take it six hours to go the length of a football field!

THE FIERCEST

There are many candidates for this category, but the **red piranha** from the Amazon River in Brazil probably wins by a fang. Renowned for their feeding frenzies, a school of hungry red piranhas can strip the flesh off a hapless victim in seconds.

THE DEADLIEST

The **box jellyfish**, also called the sea wasp, is the world's deadliest creature. The venom from just one jellyfish could kill 60 people.

THE LONGEST

The **oarfish** is the longest fish in the world. It sports a magnificent red fin that's nearly the same length as its 50-foot snakelike body. That, along with its horselike face and blue gills, accounts for it being the source of many sea serpent sightings.

"ME, QUIT? NEVER!"

It takes more than a shark to keep this kid out of the water.

Bethany Hamilton loves to surf. In fact, this teenager from Hawaii wants to be a professional surfer some day. But an early morning surf session on October 31, 2003, turned into a terrifying fight for her life. Thirteen-year-old Bethany was waiting for a wave on Kauai's

north shore when a 14-foot tiger shark attacked her. The shark bit a huge chunk out of the surfboard, along with Bethany's entire left arm. Somehow Bethany managed to paddle back to shore before passing out. By the time friends got her to the hospital, the young surfer had lost nearly 75% of her blood. But she survived…and 10 weeks later, she was out in the water again. At first, she just wanted to see if she could surf with one arm—but once she had that mastered, she started to compete again. And she won! Today Bethany travels around the world, surfing and inspiring others to go for their dreams. As Bethany says in her own words, "Me, quit? Never!"

SHARK BAIT...NOT!

Don't want to become shark bait? Here's what you need to know before you hit the surf.

Of the 375 species of sharks, only 30 are known to attack humans. There are about 70 unprovoked attacks reported worldwide every year. That's a pretty small number when you consider the millions of beach-goers who enter shark territory (shark territory being *any* part of the ocean, *anywhere*). The fact is, you're more likely to be struck by lightning than become a shark snack. But then again, if you've ever been in the ocean, you were probably within 15 feet of a shark and never knew it. So better safe than sorry, right?

1. Don't go swimming during shark feeding hours— dawn, dusk, and night.

2. Swim with friends. Sharks prefer to attack lone victims.

3. Don't get in the water if you're bleeding. Even a small cut is enough to call a shark in from the abyss.

4. Stay close to shore. You don't want a shark between you and the beach, and it will be easier for help to reach you if you are attacked.

5. Don't wear a watch or shiny jewelry (even earrings) into the water. Your jewelry looks a lot like fish scales to a shark.

6. Don't wear brightly colored bathing suits—especially yellow. Shark experts have discovered that sharks are attracted to high contrasts, including uneven tans.

7. If you see a bunch of birds diving into the water, head for the beach. The birds are diving for baitfish, and sharks love baitfish.

8. Don't go swimming where people are fishing— sharks may be fishing there, too.

9. Seeing dolphins around doesn't automatically make you safe. Large sharks hunt dolphins.

10. Don't splash a lot. A shark may mistake you for wounded prey.

11. Stay away from the shark's favorite hunting grounds—steep drop-offs near underwater cliffs or sandbars, polluted water, and murky water.

12. Don't go swimming where sharks have been spotted and never, ever try to touch one. If you see a shark, get out of the water...*fast!*

IT WAS TH-I-I-I-S BIG!

For the record, here are the
biggest creatures ever caught.

• The biggest *blue whale* was captured near the South
Shetland Islands in 1926. It was 108 feet long and
weighed 380,000 pounds.

• A *great white shark* caught off Cuba in 1945 was 21 feet
long and weighed 7,301 pounds.

• A *giant squid* captured in 1878 weighed in at 4,000
pounds, and had tentacles measuring 35 feet in length.

• The biggest *lobster* of all time (nicknamed "Mike")
was caught in 1934. This colossal crustacean weighed a
whopping 42 pounds, 7 ounces.

STINGRAY TO THE RESCUE!

*For centuries, people have written tales of
sea creatures rescuing sailors lost at sea.
But this story happens to be true.*

BOY OVERBOARD!

On January 15, 1990, 18-year-old Lottie Stevens and a friend were fishing off the island-nation of Vanuatu in the South Pacific when a fierce storm caught them by surprise. Their boat capsized, drowning Lottie's friend and leaving him clinging to the wreckage of the boat. After three days, the teenager left the floating debris and swam towards what he hoped was land. He swam for two days without getting anywhere. Exhausted, he knew he was finally about to run out of luck. Then he was suddenly lifted out of the water by a stingray! The ray was at least 15 feet long from head to tail.

RAY RIDER

At first, Lottie was terrified—stingrays aren't known to be friendly. But this giant ray carried him on its back night and day for more than two weeks. They passed safely through the shark-infested waters and rough seas until the stingray swam into the shallow waters of New Caledonia, 300 miles from Vanuatu. Lottie was lost at sea for a total of 21 days—16 of them on the back of a stingray.

ALIEN INVASION

They're here! And they're...
jellyfish?

E very autumn the seas off the west coast of Japan are invaded by millions of huge aliens who destroy fishing nets and drive off the salmon and tuna the fishermen usually catch. Although they look like something from another galaxy, these "aliens" aren't from outer space at all. They're a species of jellyfish called *Nomura's jellyfish*—giant jellies over six feet in diameter.

GIANT JELLIES

These seasonal swarms have been happening for years, but for some reason they have recently grown more intense—not just in the Sea of Japan, but around the world. *Purple jellyfish* and *lion's mane jellyfish* invaded European beaches in 2006, and *bluebottle jellies* swarmed the coasts of Australia in January 2007. Scientists think these massive swarms may be a result of global warming and overfishing.

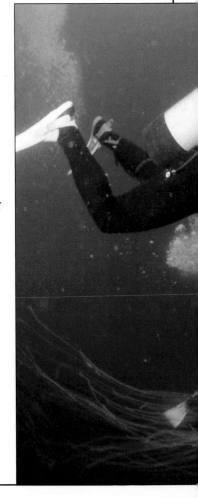

IF YOU CAN'T BEAT 'EM, EAT 'EM!

But the Japanese have come up with a way to fight back: Local chefs give cooking lessons in how to eat the jellies (recipes include salted jellyfish with cucumber and soy sauce). Or you can eat them raw, like sushi. You can have all the seconds you want, too—at 400 pounds per Nomura's jellyfish, there are always plenty of leftovers.

MISTER MOM

The most dedicated stay-at-home mom in the sea...is a dad!

Sea horses aren't really horses. They just look like them. These four-inch-long fish swim through the water upright. Their dorsal fins act like boat propellers, sending them forward. When they want to stop, they put on the brakes by grabbing hold of a piece of seaweed or coral with their curly tails.

When sea horses decide to have a family, it's the dad who does the heavy lifting. In fact, sea horses and their cousins, pipefish, are the only species on Earth in which the *dad* gets pregnant. The male sea horse has a pouch just like a kangaroo, into which the mom drops nearly 200 tiny eggs. And for the next month, that's where they grow. When it's time to give birth, the dad becomes a rocking horse: He grabs hold of a seaweed stem and rocks back and forth to launch his baby sea horses into the world.

WATER WORLD

- 71% of the Earth's surface is water.

- 97% of the Earth's water is in the ocean. Less than 1% is fresh water.

- 80% of all life lives in the ocean.

- 99% percent of the living space on the Earth is under water. (Less than 10% of that space has been explored.)

- If you were to stand at the deepest spot in the ocean, the water pressure would feel as if you were trying to lift up fifty Boeing 747s.

- There's enough gold in the ocean to give a nine-pound chunk to every person in the world.

- If you removed the salt in the ocean, you could cover all the land on Earth in a layer of salt five feet deep.

- The weight of the garbage dumped into the ocean every year is more than three times the weight of the fish caught in the same year.

- There's as much ice in Antarctica as there is water in the Atlantic Ocean.

- There are 25,000 islands in the Pacific Ocean—more than all the other islands in the other oceans combined.

- What's the tallest mountain on Earth? It's mostly underwater. Mauna Kea in Hawaii rises 33,465 feet from the ocean floor, beating Mt. Everest by more than 3,000 feet.

MORE SHARK FACTS

> Sharks never get cancer. Scientists hope to discover the shark's secret defense to help us create anti-cancer drugs.

> The *swell shark* from New Zealand barks like a dog.

> Bull sharks are the only sharks that can live in both salt and fresh water. There's a lake in Nicaragua that's full of them.

> Here are some of the things that have been found inside a shark's stomach: an alarm clock, an unopened bottle of wine, a drum, a bicycle, a treasure chest, a suit of armor, and a torpedo.

OFF THE DEEP END

Q: *What happened to the fishing boat that sank in piranha-infested waters?*

A: It came back with a skeleton crew.

Q: If they made a movie starring the Loch Ness monster and the great white shark from *Jaws*, what would the movie be called?

A: *Loch Jaws.*

Q: *Why is it so easy to weigh fish?*

A: They have their own scales.

Q: *What sits at the bottom of the sea and shivers?*

A: A nervous wreck.

Q: *What sea animal can be adjusted to play music?*

A: The tune-a fish!

THE BLOOP

*There's something very **loud deep in the ocean**.*

DID YOU HEAR THAT?

The ocean is a noisy place. Undersea volcanoes rumble, whales sing, dolphins whistle, and shrimp snap. Scientists have been listening to the sounds for years through a network of underwater microphones. But researchers were startled in 1997 when they heard a noise in the Pacific Ocean, louder than anything they'd ever heard before (the microphones that picked up the sound were over 3,000 miles apart). It sounded like this: "BLOOP."

Was it manmade? No, no one has ever made a machine —not even a bomb—as loud as the Bloop. Was it a whale? No. Blue whales are the loudest animals on the planet, but the Bloop made their call sound like a "peep."

So what was it? Nobody knows.

SURF'S UP–WAY UP!

Ken Bradshaw holds the record for surfing the biggest wave, an 85-footer at Waimea Bay, Hawaii, on January 20, 1988. Giant waves break as far as two miles from shore so surfers like Ken usually get towed out from shore on Jet-Skis. Some even drop in from a helicopter!

This surfer is taking a giant wave in the Big Wave Invitational surfing championship in Waimea Bay, Hawaii, in 2004.

DAUNTLESS DOLPHIN

On August 20, 2000, Davide Ceci was boating with his father, Emanuele Ceci, in the Adriatic Sea near Manfredonia, Italy, when he fell out of the boat. His father was busy steering the boat and didn't see the 14-year-old go overboard. Davide didn't know how to swim; the last thing he saw before sinking beneath the waves was the boat sailing away. Then Davide felt something large push him up to the surface. It was a dolphin. And amazingly, Davide knew this particular dolphin by name. "Felippo" had shown up in the bay two years earlier and had become the unofficial mascot of their seaside community. The boy held on tightly while Felippo chased down Mr. Ceci's boat, then swam alongside until Davide's dad was able to reach down and pull his son to safety.

SCUBA DO!

Sailor, scientist, inventor, explorer, filmmaker, and TV host, Jacques Cousteau made it possible for humans to explore the world under the sea.

How long can you hold your breath underwater? Most people can only hold it for a minute or two. And until 1943, that was the longest most divers could spend under the surface. That's when French naval officer Jacques Cousteau and engineer Emile Gagnan invented a device to let divers breathe underwater for hours. They called it the *aqualung*, and it wasn't long before he started using it to get an "up close" look at the astounding world of undersea life.

The experience changed him forever. A few years later he set out on his research ship, the *Calypso*, to explore the oceans of the world. Cousteau visited every body of water on Earth, from the Arctic Ocean to the Mississippi River. He revealed the amazing beauty of the ocean depths in his award-winning films *The Silent World* and *World Without Sun* and in his 1970s television show, *The Undersea World of Jacques Cousteau*. By the time he died in 1997, Cousteau had done more to teach people about the oceans than anyone who's ever lived. Best of all, he gave all of us the opportunity to become underwater explorers—just like him.

DIVING DOWN

Here's a quick guide to the history of deep sea diving.

2500 BC—A Greek named Scyllis invents the breathing tube. While being held prisoner by the Persians, he discovers their attack plans and jumps overboard. That night, using a reed as a snorkel, he swims underwater from ship to ship and sabotages the Persian fleet.

1535—Guglielmo de Lorena makes the first practical diving bell—an upside-down pot lowered into the water, trapping air that divers can breathe for a short time.

1690—John Lethbridge invents the first "diving suit," an enclosed wooden cylinder with leather sleeves. To everyone's surprise, it works.

1788—John Smeaton makes a *better* diving bell. This one has a hand pump to get fresh air. Within 10 years, his bell is used all over Europe and America.

1837—Augustus Siebe invents the first rubber diving suit sealed to an attached diving helmet. This type of diving suit is still used today.

1865—Two Frenchmen invent the "Aerophore"—an air tank strapped to the diver's back and connected by a mouthpiece. It inspires Jules Verne to include one in his novel, *20,000 Leagues Under the Sea.*

1917—The Mark V Diving Helmet becomes the official diving helmet of the U.S. Navy. (It still is.)

1930—William Beebe sets a depth record of 1,426 feet in a round steel ball called a *bathysphere* attached to a mother ship by a steel cable.

1930—Guy Gilpatric invents rubber goggles. Snorkels and fins are already in use.

1943—Jacques-Yves Cousteau and Emil Gagnan invent the *aqualung*, the first practical SCUBA gear.

1954—Georges Houot and Pierre-Willm take the newly invented *bathyscaphe*, a submarine-like submersible, 13,287 feet under the sea—a new record.

1960—Jacques Piccard and Don Walsh pilot the bathyscaphe *Trieste* 35,820 feet into the Mariana Trench. It is the absolute bottom of the ocean, and no one will ever go deeper.

SWIM SCHOOL

You probably know that fish swim in schools. But did you know a group of sharks is called a shiver? Try to match each sea creature with its group.

1. Starfish
2. Jellyfish
3. Turtles
4. Oysters
5. Dolphins
6. Seahorses
7. Eels
8. Whales
9. Rainbow Fish
10. Crabs
11. Goldfish
12. Sardines
13. Herring
14. Flying fish

A. Glide
B. Gam
C. Bale
D. Smack
E. Swarm
F. Army
G. Troubling
H. Colony
I. Herd
J. Party
K. Bed
L. Cast
M. Family
N. Pod

DID YOU KNOW?

A school of fish can also be called a *shoal*, a *haul*, a *draught*, a *run*, a *catch*, a *flutter*, a *cast*, a *throw*, or a *warp* of fish!

ANSWERS: 1-H, 2-D, 3-C, 4-K, 5-N, 6-I, 7-E, 8-B, 9-J, 10-L, 11-G, 12-M, 13-F, 14-A.

IT'S SLIMY!
IT'S DISGUSTING!
IT'S A HAGFISH!

This slimy eel can tie itself in knots!

Hagfish are the vultures of the sea. They live in the mucky goop that covers the ocean floor, feeding on the bodies of dead fish that sink down from the surface. The way they like to eat the carcasses is truly gross: They crawl inside the body and eat their way out. These primitive fish haven't changed for over 300 million years. Hagfish are nearly blind, and have three hearts but no jaws, stomach, or bones. They are also called *slime eels*, and here's why: When another

predator grabs them, they cover themselves with slime—gobs of it. A hagfish can crank out a gallon of the stuff in seconds. Then it ties itself in a knot, which usually lets it slip out of the predator's grip. Hagfish also use the knot trick to clean off their slime once they're free. And if that doesn't do the trick—they sneeze!

REAL MONSTERS?

Meet Oregon's most famous sea serpents.

Fishermen have been sighting sea serpents off the Oregon coast for more than 100 years. Two of them have become so well known that they have their own names: Colossal Claude and Marvin the Monster.

COLOSSAL CLAUDE

This monster was first seen in 1934 swimming near the mouth of the Columbia River. Eyewitness L.A. Larson described it as "eight feet long, with a big round body, a mean-looking tail, and an evil, snaky head." Three years later, Claude was spotted again by another person, who described the creature as being a long, tan-colored, hairy monster with a head like a horse. Other fishermen saw Claude, too, but they were reluctant to get too close for fear the beast would flip over their boats. But the schooner *Arpo* sailed within a few feet and got a good look at the monster as it snatched a big halibut off the boat's fishing line. According to Captain Chris Anderson, the monster had "glassy eyes, and a head like a camel." Even odder was the fact that Colossal Claude seemed to be covered in *fur*.

MARVIN THE MONSTER

When this creature made its first appearance in 1963, it scared the wetsuits off some oil company divers exploring an offshore canyon. Fortunately, the divers were able to film the 15-foot-long monster and show the movie to marine biologists at universities in California, Washington, and Texas. Marvin the Monster has popped up many times since then, and film of him swimming around underwater has been shown on television. But scientists still have no idea what kind of creature Marvin —or Claude, for that matter—might be.

STOP THAT LOBSTER!

*It's not a good idea to eat the claw
that saved your wallet...*

A LUCKY CATCH

One hot August evening in 2006, Paul Westlake of Milehouse, England, decided to jump into the ocean to cool off. When he got out, Paul realized that he'd lost his wallet somewhere in the water. It was too dark to dive down to find it, so he figured it was gone forever.

A few days later, a local diver spotted a lobster scurrying along the ocean bottom...carrying a wallet in one of its claws. The diver caught the lobster (and the wallet), and went home. That night, over a delicious lobster dinner, he thumbed through the contents of the wallet and found a hair salon appointment card for Paul Westlake. When he called the next day, the hair stylist thought it was a prank. But when the diver brought the wallet by, the salon notified Paul, who was soon reunited with his soggy wallet. Paul never got to thank the diver (he had walked away without identifying himself), and he felt awful when he found out the lobster had been eaten. "I have never eaten a lobster," he said, "and now I never will."

RUBBER DUCKIES OVERBOARD!

In 1992 there was a shipping accident that spilled 29,000 rubber ducks and other bath toys into the middle of the Pacific Ocean. The little yellow ducks floated on the ocean for almost a year, just going with the flow...until one day a few thousand washed up on the shores of Alaska. Many more continued their journey north through the Bering Straits and were frozen in the Arctic icepack. By 2003—11 years later—these frozen adventurers had finally made their way across the Pole to the North Atlantic and were spotted bobbing merrily off beaches from Maine to Massachusetts.

DAVY JONES' LOCKER

Uncle John wants to know—who the heck is Davy Jones?

For centuries, when a sailor was drowned at sea, sailors would say, "He's gone to Davy Jones' Locker," meaning he was buried at the bottom of the sea. But where did the phrase come from? The first written reference to Davy Jones was in the 1751 novel *The Adventures of Peregrine Pickle*, where he was described as a real sea devil with saucer-like eyes, three rows of teeth, horns, a tail, and blue smoke coming out of his nose. The 2006 movie *Pirates of the Caribbean: Dead Man's Chest* presented Davy Jones as an evil mutant mix of human and octopus. But how did he get the name Davy Jones? One theory says "Davy" comes from St. David, the patron saint of sailors, and "Jones" is from Jonah, the Biblical seaman who got swallowed by a whale, and whose name still means bad luck to sailors.

But there's another legend. According to this story, Davy Jones was a 16th century Welsh innkeeper with a nasty side business: He would get sailors so drunk that they'd pass out. Then he'd stick them in his ale locker (a room used to store barrels of ale) until some friends arrived with a cart to haul the unconscious sailors to the nearest ship that was short a few crewmen. Jones got a tidy fee for each "delivery." As for the drunken sailor, he'd wake up when the ship was far out to sea, with a headache…and the shock of his life.

HERE BE TREASURE!

Tales of pirate gold, lost and found...

DOUBLE TROUBLE. Ever dream of finding buried pirate booty? Travel to the Costa Rican island of Cocos and you may get a two-for-one. In 1818, somewhere in the island's tree-covered hills, Benito "Bloody Sword" Bonito buried a load of Spanish gold worth $300 million. In 1820 another pirate, William Thompson, hijacked the legendary Treasure of Lima (the wealth of more than 50 churches in the Peruvian capital), and stashed it on Cocos. Since then, hundreds of treasure hunters have scoured the island—including President Franklin Roosevelt—but no one has ever found either hoard.

HAPPY ENDING? Captain "Black Sam" Bellamy's ship, the *Whydah*, sank off the coast of New England in 1717. Along with the 143 pirates who drowned was a fortune in gold and silver. Deep-sea diver Barty Clifford searched for 15 years without success, but in 1984 he finally found the ship. So far, more than 100,000 treasure items, including chests of gold and silver doubloons, have been pulled from the wreck of the *Whydah*. Clifford is certain that most of the treasure is still lost in the sand, waiting to be found.

BATTLE, BARF, AND BULLION

Whale vomit is as rare as gold,
and worth a whole lot more!

THE BATTLE

Somewhere down deep in the ocean, two of the world's largest predators will face each other today in a battle of life and death. On one side is the bull sperm whale—60 feet long, 65 tons, with a mouthful of razor-sharp teeth and a nasty attitude. A sperm whale can hold its breath up to two hours while it dives more than a mile below the surface to hunt for its favorite food—the giant squid. The monster squid are as big as the whales that hunt them. With a sharp beak, sucker-lined arms, and two whip-like feeding tentacles, a giant squid is no pushover. No one has ever witnessed a fight

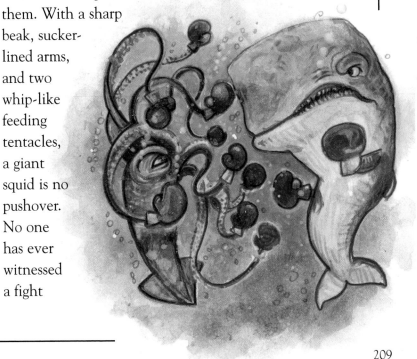

between these deep-sea behemoths, but battle scars are visible on the whales when they surface—deep gashes from the beaks, and round welts left by the suckers. Sometimes the squid escapes, disappearing behind a cloud of dark ink. If the whale wins, it swallows the squid whole. But the squid gets revenge: Its beak is indigestible, which irritates the whale's stomach until sooner or later it barfs it out.

THE BARF

For most creatures, that would be the end of the story. But not the sperm whale. The black gooey vomit drifts along the ocean currents, soaking up the sun. Over time it hardens into a sweet-smelling, waxy lump known as *ambergris*. Or, as sailors have long called it, "floating gold."

THE BULLION

Ambergris has been prized for thousands of years. The Chinese thought it came from sleeping dragons drooling on sunny seashore rocks, so they called it "dragon's spittle perfume." The Dutch and English used to breakfast on ambergris and eggs. It has been used as medicine, a spice for food and wine and, most significantly, as an ingredient in making fine perfume. It's been cut up into round balls, polished, and worn as "whale pearls." Ambergris is so valuable that just one gram of it (.035 of an ounce) can fetch up to $20. However, it comes in so many different colors, shapes, and textures that most beachcombers don't know real ambergris when they find it.

UNCLE JOHN'S AMBERGRIS TEST

In case you're not sure whether to show that weird goop you found on the beach to your science teacher...

WHAT YOU'LL NEED

1 batch of possible whale barf found on beach

1 needle, 1 match, and 1 candle (and adult supervision)

HOW TO DO IT

1. Heat the needle

2. Briefly touch the whale barf with the hot needle.

3. Real ambergris will melt instantly. A black oily residue will ooze from the pricked spot, and a puff of musky-smelling smoke will appear.

Dorothy Ferreira of Long Island, New York, got this piece of (maybe) ambergris as a gift in 2006. She's having it tested to see if it's the real thing. If it is, it may be worth $18,000!

HEY, LET GO OF MY BOAT!

The skies were clear, the wind crisp. Olivier de Kersauson's sleek racing boat was speeding through the deep ocean off the island of Madeira in the South Atlantic. The veteran French sailor and his crew were just beginning an around-the-world race to win the prestigious Jules Verne Trophy, when all at once they got the surprise of their lives. De Kersauson was below deck when the hull shuddered and the boat slowed down abruptly. Looking out the porthole, he saw a giant tentacle thicker than his leg. Rushing up on deck, he found two other tentacles wrapped around the rudder. A giant squid 24 feet long had grabbed hold of the yacht and wouldn't let go. Luckily for de Kersauson, he didn't have to fight off the monster—as soon as the boat came to a stop, the giant squid released the boat and slid beneath the waves. "We didn't have anything to scare off this beast, so I don't know what we would have done if it hadn't let go," de Kersauson said later. "We weren't going to attack it with our penknives."

"HA! YOU MISSED ME!"

Diving for abalone—a shellfish prized for its delicate flavor—isn't the easiest job in the world. The water is cold and murky, and predators prowl the shadows. Since abalone divers stay underwater for six or seven hours at a stretch, they have to wear lead-weighted vests to stay submerged. For one Australian diver, that vest saved his life.

Eric Nerhus was diving off New South Wales, Australia, in 2007 when a 10-foot great white shark decided to eat him—head first. The bite crushed Eric's mask and broke his nose, but what came next was worse. Within seconds, his head and shoulders were completely inside the shark's throat. But Eric had no intention of being shark lunch. A black belt in karate, he used his free arm to punch at the shark's eyes and gills until it spit him out. But it was his vest that saved his life—it protected him from the shark's teeth like a coat of armor. Lucky Eric walked away with cuts and scrapes, and bite marks on his chest. (The vest had to be thrown away.)

S. O. S.

Ten things you can do to Save Our Seas.

It's only recently that humans have come to understand how much we need a healthy ocean to survive. The ocean makes most of the oxygen we breathe. It cleans the water we drink. It gives us food and even medicine. But we've haven't taken good care of it—we dump our garbage into it, and we've fished some species to near-extinction, destroying coral reefs in the process. Today the ocean is in trouble. But if we work together, we can help stop the damage we've done...and we have to start right away.

AT THE BEACH

1. Keep the ocean clean. Take your trash home with you, even if there's a trashcan on the beach.

2. Protect the sand dunes. Don't walk or play on the dunes. They help prevent erosion.

3. Protect the wildlife. Avoid nesting areas, and don't bother or chase sea birds or animals.

4. Protect the reefs. Reefs are *very* fragile. Just one touch can harm a reef—walking on one can kill it.

5. Fish smart. Catch what you can eat and release the rest. Take all fishing lines and nets home with you, even the broken ones. Birds and fish can get tangled in them and die.

AT HOME

6. Don't let go of that balloon! Sea turtles mistake balloons (and plastic bags) for their favorite food, jellyfish, which can be a fatal mistake.

7. Shop smart. Only buy things that you really want or need. The less stuff we throw away, the less stuff that gets dumped in the ocean.

8. Eat sustainable food. Eat fish and shellfish caught or farmed in ways that support the oceans in the long-term. Go organic—pesticides and fertilizers from traditional farming are poisoning the ocean.

9. Reduce your greenhouse gas footprint. When you walk, ride your bike, turn off the lights, and recycle, you produce fewer greenhouse gasses. That helps reduce global warming, and helps keep the oceans at temperatures that support wildlife.

10. Learn everything you can about the ocean. Share what you've learned with your friends. They might be inspired to help protect the ocean, too.

And...on June 8th, celebrate World Ocean Day.

POLAR OPPOSITES

Some chillin' facts...

NORTH POLE

• The Arctic is a frozen ocean surrounded by continents.

• The Arctic is named after the Big Dipper constellation, also know as the Great Bear. In Greek, both are called called *Arktikos*.

• The pack ice in the Arctic Ocean is an average of 10–12 feet thick.

• Polar bears, walruses, beluga, and narwhals are found only in the Arctic.

• Trees and shrubs grow along the southern edges of the Arctic.

• Lots of land animals live in the Arctic—arctic foxes, rabbits, caribou, elk, and reindeer, to name a few.

• Even if all the ice in the Arctic Ocean melted, the oceans wouldn't rise. That's because ice floats on the ocean and displaces its weight in seawater. Think of a full glass of iced tea: When the ice cubes melt, does the level rise? No, it stays the same (unless, of course, you've been drinking the tea).

POLAR OPPOSITES

...to help you keep your poles straight.

SOUTH POLE

- The Antarctic is a continent surrounded by ocean.

- The word *Antarctic* means "opposite of Arctic."

- The ice sheets covering the continent of Antarctica have an average depth of 1.5 miles.

- Emperor, Adelie, Chinstrap, and Gentoo penguins live only in the Antarctic.

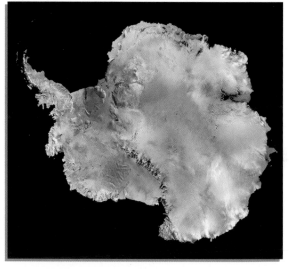

The continent of Antarctica, seen from space.

- No trees or bushes grow in the Antarctic— only moss, algae, and lichens. Because it's so cold, some plants actually grow *inside* the rocks.

- The only land animals that live in the Antarctic are midges, mites, ticks, and nematode worms.

- Because Antarctica is a continent, if all of its ice sheets melted, the ice would flow off the land into the sea. That would cause the ocean to rise by 200 feet.

SEALS

Go ahead...clap your flippers and bark.

WHAT HAS A TORPEDO-SHAPED BODY, 4 FLIPPERS, AND NO EARS?

You guessed it—a seal. Its torpedo-like body allows it to zip through the water at speeds of up to 25 mph, and dive down 1,000 feet. Its two front flippers have claws and are used for steering; the rear flippers are its propellers.

WHAT'S THE BIGGEST SEAL?

It's the elephant seal, of course, which can weigh as much as 5,000 pounds.

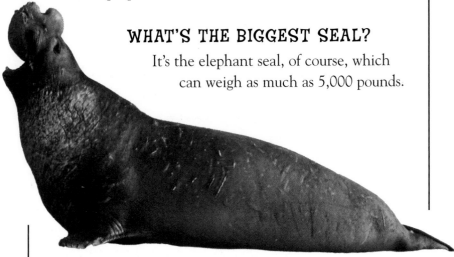

WHAT'S THE SMALLEST SEAL?

An adult ringed seal tips the scales at only 110 pounds.

WHAT DO SEALS LIKE TO EAT?

Krill, squid, and fish—but not necessarily in that order.

WHERE DO SEALS LIVE?

Anywhere they want to. Really. Seals live in all of the oceans of the world. They even pop up in freshwater lakes, such as Lake Baikal in Russia. But the majority can be found near Antarctica and the Arctic Circle.

HOW MANY KINDS OF SEALS ARE THERE?

There are 18 seal species, which include the harbor seal, the bearded seal, the crabeater seal, the harp seal, the spotted seal, and the hooded seal. There used to be a 19th species—the Caribbean monk seal—but it was last seen in 1952. It's now thought to be extinct.

WHAT IS THE MOST FEROCIOUS SEAL?

The leopard seal wins this award. A predator that gets its name from its black spots, it can grow to be 12 feet long. It has long, sharp teeth and a head that looks like a reptile's. A leopard seal likes to lie in wait under the ice in Antarctica for its dinner to come along. Then it bursts out of the water, snapping up penguins, smaller seals, and sometimes taking a bite at a polar explorer or two.

FOLLOW THAT FIN!

For more than 20 years, a dolphin named Pelorus Jack guided sailing ships through dangerous waters.

Hundreds of shipwrecks litter the sea floor between New Zealand's North and South Islands, victims of the treacherous rocks and swirling currents of a narrow channel known as the French Pass. So when the sailing ship *Brindle* entered the channel in 1888, the sailors were understandably alarmed when they heard a shout from a crew member. Had they run aground? No, but to their amazement, they saw a Risso's dolphin swimming alongside the ship.

GOING MY WAY?

Risso's are open-ocean dolphins that prefer the company of their own pod, not people. To see one at all was rare; to see one near a ship was very unusual. What was even more odd was the dolphin's behavior: It wasn't playing in the bow wake, as dolphins commonly do. Instead, it seemed to be *leading* the ship through the channel.

And when the *Brindle* set out on its return trip, the dolphin was waiting at the mouth of the channel, ready to guide the ship safely back. The grateful sailors nicknamed their finny guide Pelorus Jack, after the *pelorus*, a compass used to get one's bearings on the open ocean.

For the next 24 years, Pelorus Jack guided ships safely through the channel. The dolphin was so reliable that ships would wait for him to appear before going forward.

The dolphin's fame grew and people flocked to see him, including authors Rudyard Kipling and Mark Twain. Then in 1904, a drunken passenger on a ship called the *Penguin* shot the dolphin. Pelorus Jack swam away, leaving a trail of blood behind him. No one knew if Jack was alive or dead. Two weeks later, the dolphin reappeared and took up his usual post. But Jack never led the *Penguin* through the channel again. The shooting incident caused an outrage, and a law was passed making it illegal to shoot a dolphin in New Zealand waters.

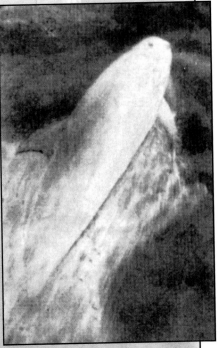

One of the few existing photos of Jack.

GOODBYE, OLD FRIEND

Five years after the shooting incident, on February 12, 1909, the *Penguin* sank on the rocks of French Pass. It was the only ship lost in the channel during Pelorus Jack's career.

Pelorus Jack guided his last ship on April 12, 1912. He disappeared shortly after that, and probably died of old age. Grateful New Zealanders declared a day of national mourning to honor him.

FUNGHI

No, not a mushroom, but the famous Dolphin of Dingle.

Funghi is a bottlenose dolphin who swam into the Bay of Dingle one day—and never left. Since 1983, Funghi has entertained visitors to Dingle, a quaint town on the west coast of Ireland, every day of the week, escorting boats in and out of the harbor. He surfs the bow wakes of the boats, and even lets swimmers come up and play with him. The dolphin's presence has become so predictable that a huge tourist industry has grown up around him, making Funghi famous all over the world.

LONG-ARMED RESCUE

Can't reach that hard-to-get spot?
Call the world's tallest man!

On December 13, 2006, veterinarians at Royal Jidi Ocean World in Fushon, China, found themselves facing a tricky problem: Two mischievous dolphins had swallowed some large pieces of plastic that had been left by their pool. The vet couldn't anesthetize them and remove the objects surgically because, unlike most animals, dolphins can't breathe if they're not awake.

The vet tried to pull out the plastic pieces by reaching down the dolphins' throats, but his arm was too short. They needed someone with a *really* long arm. Enter Bao Xishun, the World's Tallest Man. According to the *Guinness Book of Records*, he's 7 feet, 8 inches tall. His arms are 3 feet, 4 inches long—long enough to reach down and pull out the dangerous pieces of plastic.

Each dolphin was held down by a dozen keepers, and towels were wrapped around their jaws to keep the dolphins' sharp teeth from scratching Bao's arm. The operation was over in seconds. Good thing, too, because the plastic had been in the dolphins' stomachs for over two weeks. The vets said they would have died soon if the long-armed surgery hadn't worked!

GENTLE GIANTS

These huge sharks are the "vacuum cleaners" of the sea!

S ome of the largest fish live by eating the smallest food. Meet the giant sharks: These easy-going guys have nothing in common with their fiercer cousins. They're "filter feeders"—they swim along with their mouths wide open, scooping up huge amounts of water which they strain through long bristles called *gill rakers*. They flush out the water and keep the stuff they like: plankton, fish eggs, and tiny shrimp known as *krill*.

BASKING SHARK

The basking shark is the world's second largest fish—it can grow up to 33 feet long and weigh 8,000 pounds.

The basking shark also has hundreds of tiny teeth inside its mouth… but they're of little or no use. These filter-feeders hang out near the surface of the ocean, either alone or in schools of up to 100 sharks.

WHALE SHARK

Whale sharks are the world's biggest fish. They can grow up to 46 feet long and weigh more than 47,000 pounds. (Remember, they're not whales—they're *fish*.) The whale shark has 3,000 teeth in its cavernous mouth, but the teeth are tiny and harmless. Whale sharks are found in all the warm oceans of the world.

MEGAMOUTH

The first mega-mouth shark was discovered in Hawaii in 1976. Since then, only 38 more have been seen, making the megamouth one

of the rarest sharks in the world. This weird-looking creature has an oversized head with big rubbery lips and a huge mouth, lined with 50 rows of tiny teeth. The largest megamouth on record measured 16 feet long and weighed 2,205 pounds.

SHARK JOKES

For those of you who like a little bite in your humor.

Q: *What happens when you cross a great white shark with a cow?*

A: I don't know—but whatever you do, don't milk it.

Q: *What does a shark eat with peanut butter?*

A: Jellyfish.

Q: *Why do sharks swim only in saltwater?*

A: Because pepper water would make them sneeze.

Q: *What happened to the shark who swallowed a bunch of keys?*

A: He got lockjaw.

Q: *How can you tell a boy shark from a girl shark?*

A: You give it a fish. If *he* eats it, it's a boy…if *she* eats it, it's a girl.

Q: *Why don't sharks eat clowns?*

A: They taste funny.

Q: *What do you get from a bad-tempered shark?*

A: As far away as possible!

Q: *Where do fish go when they want to borrow money?*

A: A loan shark.

Q: *What do you get when you cross a big fish with an electric wire?*

A: An electric shark.

MESSAGE IN A BOTTLE

You never know what you'll find washed up on shore.

LUCKY FIND

The most incredible "message in a bottle" story of all time took place in San Francisco in 1949. Jack Wurm was having a rough time: He'd lost his job and run out of money. Hopeless and depressed, he took a walk along the beach, trying to figure out what to do next. Then he noticed a bottle with a piece of paper in it sticking out of the sand. He picked it up and pried off

the cork. What he found inside was almost too good to be true—a signed will that read, "I leave my entire estate to the lucky person who finds this bottle." The will belonged to the late Daisy Singer Alexander, heiress to the Singer sewing machine fortune. She had thrown the bottle in the Thames River in England 12 years earlier. The bottle and the will had drifted all the way around the world to San Francisco, and to Jack Wurm—who became a millionaire overnight!

GUESS WHO?

Some fish do whatever they can to not look like a fish.

LEAFY SEA DRAGON

These relatives of the sea horse look like floating pieces of seaweed—a perfect disguise for hiding among the patches of kelp-covered rocks where they make their home in cool waters off the

coast of Australia. Their mouths work like a drinking straw: When the tiny shrimp they like to eat swim by, leafy sea dragons slurp them up like a milk shake.

TASSELED WOBBEGONG

This bizarre-looking creature likes to bury its flattened body against the sea floor and wait for lunch to swim by. Its amazing camouflage of patterns and colors make it

look like leftover shag carpet…which is why it's also called a carpet shark. This native of the South Pacific hides out in caves, or rests on coral reefs down to depths of 130 feet.

Now you see him...

BIG BLUE (DAY) OCTOPUS

Say hello to one of the supreme masters of sea disguise. Not only can a big blue octopus change color, it can alter the texture of its skin to look just like the reef rock it lives on. That's a great survival skill for a creature that hunts in broad daylight. While diving off the coast of Hawaii, one marine biologist watched a big blue change its look 1,000 times in seven hours.

...now you don't!

IT WAS TH-I-I-I-S BIG!

More of the biggest sea creatures ever found.

• The largest *leatherback turtle* ever recorded was 10 feet from tip to tail, and weighed in at 2,019 pounds.

• A *trumpet conch* collected in 1979 off the coast of Australia was 30 inches long and 40 inches around. The snail inside it weighed 40 pounds, making it the largest marine snail on record.

• The largest *sea star* was found in the North Pacific Ocean. It weighed 11 pounds and was nearly 38 inches in diameter.

• The largest *clam* ever collected was taken in 1917 from Australia's Great Barrier Reef. It was 49 inches long and weighed 579 pounds. An even bigger clam was discovered in 1965, measuring 53 inches in length. But the divers left it on the reef to keep on growing!

• In 1934 a Filipino diver found a huge *pearl* 10 inches in diameter and weighing 14 pounds. Today the pearl, now known as the Pearl of Lao-tze, is worth $40 million.

SEA SQUIRT

Talk about losing your mind. This guy eats his own brain!

Sea squirts are *tunicates*—animals made up of a simple tube, which they use as a siphon to suck in passing plankton. Unlike worms and jellyfish, sea squirts have a backbone, which makes them vertebrates, just like us. In fact, scientists think sea squirts may have been one of the first vertebrates to exist on the planet. In the early stages of its development, a sea squirt embryo looks much like any other vertebrate's embryo, whether it's a rat, fish, lion, or human. And baby sea squirts are born with a brain, just like people. So you could say that the sea squirt is our distant cousin.

The sea squirt does something unique in the sea world. A baby sea squirt uses its brain to pick out a permanent place to live. Once it's found a spot of rock to attach itself to, it doesn't need that brain anymore—so the sea squirt eats it. Really. It absorbs its simple brain back into its body and goes on merrily with its simple life— sucking in, blowing out, sucking in, blowing out…

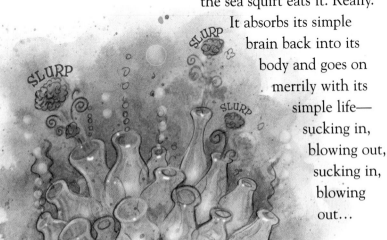

BIG MOUTHS

What do these three fish have in common? They can all swallow prey larger than themselves.

GULPER EEL

This deep-sea fish isn't much more than a giant mouth

with a tail so long that it sometimes gets tied in knots. The average gulper is about two feet long, although some can grow to six feet. Their huge mouths are hinged loosely so they can open them wide like a net. This lets them "gulp" animals much larger than themselves. Conveniently, a gulper's stomach stretches out to handle a "biggie size" meal.

Gulpers live way down deep in the ocean, anywhere from 3,000–10,000 feet.

HAIRY ANGLER

The *hairy angler* was only recently discovered when one drifted into range of a BBC camera during the filming of the documentary *The Blue Planet* in 2003. The hairy angler's Latin name is *Caulophryne polynema*, which means "stalked toad with many filaments"—a good description of this peculiar fish. Its beach ball-sized body is covered in long antennae called *neuromasts* which pick out the movements of any prey foolish enough to come close to its mouth, which is full of fanged teeth. Like the gulper eel, it can loosen its jaws to swallow prey bigger than it is, and digest them in its expandable stomach. Hairy anglers haunt the black waters of the Atlantic Ocean down to 8,000 feet.

FANGTOOTH

The *fangtooth's* teeth are so big that it can't close its mouth. In fact, it has the largest teeth of any fish in the ocean its size. So it's a good thing this guy is only six inches long. Also called an ogrefish, the fang-tooth's squat body is covered with small prickly scales. This is a tough critter: Able to withstand incredible pressures and near-freezing temperatures, the fangtooth can be found all over the world at incredible depths of down to 16,000 feet.

THE SALTY SEA

It's big. It's wet. And you can't drink it.

Why do lakes and rivers have fresh water, while the ocean has salty water? Doesn't all that fresh river water flow right into the ocean? Yes, but on its way to the ocean, that water sucks tons of minerals and chemicals out of the land. By the time it enters the big blue sea, it's full of iron, calcium, magnesium, potassium, silica, nitrate, chloride, and...sodium (salt). When this mineral-packed water meets the ocean, the sea life makes good use of it. Plankton use the silica to make their shells. Shrimp, lobsters, and crabs use the calcium to make their claws and armor. Lots of sea creatures use *some* of the minerals in the water, but *none* use sodium, so it stays in the water.

So how much salt is in the ocean? Four billion tons of it run into the ocean each year. For every ton of seawater, there's about 70 pounds of salt mixed in. Some seawater is saltier than others. The Red Sea is the saltiest because it lies in a hot, dry region, between Egypt and Saudi Arabia, where the intense heat causes evaporation; as more water is drawn into the atmosphere, more salt is left behind. The Arctic Ocean is the least salty for the same reason. The colder the ocean air, the less evaporation and the less salt.

SNOT BALLS!

How do creatures at the bottom of the sea get food?

There's a mystery that's puzzled marine biologists for years. They knew that the ocean bottom is crawling with creatures who feed on sediment that settles down to the ocean floor. But they also knew that the sediment contained barely half the food needed to support the population of bottom creatures. So where do those bottom feeders get the rest of their food?

The answer lies near the surface, where little animals called *giant larvaceans* make homes for themselves out of their own mucus. The tadpole-sized creatures spin a mucus web about three feet wide, and hide in the middle of it while it snags their food for them. The web works for about 24 hours before it gets clogged. Then the larvacean jumps ship and starts spinning a new web. The old web sinks all the way to the bottom of the sea, picking up little animals and bits of algae on the way. When these glops of snotty goop finally hit the bottom, the creatures down there gobble them up. And scientists believe these "sinkers" account for half the food on the ocean floor!

THAR' SHE BLOWS!

Whew! Gotta cut down on the plankton!

id you know that whales fart? It's true! Like humans, they are mammals, so scientists have long figured that whales would pass gas just like every other animal in the world. Now there's proof. Marine biologists in the Antarctic were tracking Minke whales (a relatively small whale, weighing about 5,000 pounds and is 25 feet long) when one of them (a whale, that is) cut a big one. The bubble was more than six feet in diameter when it popped up at the surface near the bow of the ship. The stench was so bad that the scientists frantically ran to the back of the ship to get away.

Now, what Uncle John wants to know is—who pulled the whale's flipper?

GHOST SHIPS

The ocean is huge. Ships are tiny.
Sometimes they get lost...forever.

THE *MARY CELESTE*

There were 10 people on board the *Mary Celeste* when the 103-foot sailing freighter left New York harbor on November 7, 1872. Captain Ben Briggs, his wife, his two-year-old daughter, and a crew of seven were bound for Genoa, Italy, carrying a cargo of rubbing alcohol. A month later another ship, the *Dei Gratia*, spotted the *Mary Celeste* drifting near the Azores, several hundred miles off the coast of Portugal. When the crew boarded the ship, they found it deserted. There was no sign of a struggle or evidence of any emergency. The kitchen and living quarters were all neatly stowed away. The captain's logbook was open on his desk, with the last entry dated from a week before. It was as if everyone on board had just gotten up and walked off the ship. No trace of Captain Briggs, his family, or the crew was ever found.

THE *OCTAVIA*

The whaling ship *Herald* was sailing off the coast of Greenland in 1775 when it spotted a derelict ship floating among the icebergs. The whalers promptly sent a boat and crew over to see what had happened. There they found the *Octavia*'s crew below deck—frozen solid and perfectly preserved. The captain was still at his table in his cabin, hunched over his logbook, his pen still in his hand. Afraid that the sailors had died of a plague, the whalers hurried back to their own ship, taking only the *Octavia*'s logbook to prove they'd seen the vessel. The last entry in the logbook was dated 1762, which meant that the *Octavia* had been drifting around the Arctic Ocean for 13 years!

THE *OURANG MEDAN*

Late in July 1947, an American freighter named the *Silver Star* was navigating the Strait of Malacca off the coast of Indonesia when its radioman picked up frantic distress signals from the Dutch freighter *Ourang Medan*. The badly garbled messages rambled about the captain and crew having died mysteriously. There was a burst of gibberish in Morse code, followed by an ominous, "I die." Then the signals stopped. It took the *Silver Star* several hours to reach the *Ourang Medan*. When a boarding party was sent over to investigate, they found a truly ghastly sight: The crew and officers lay in grotesque positions, their eyes wide open, arms thrown out to the sides, looks of terror gripping their dead faces. The ship's dog was dead, too, its teeth bared as if threatened by some unknown menace. Weirdest of all was the sudden chill the rescue team felt while exploring the boiler room—even though the outside temperature was over 100° F. The captain of the *Silver Star* decided to tow the *Ourang Medan* to the nearest port. While the crew was attaching tow lines, smoke began to pour out of the ghost ship. The *Silver Star* barely had time to cut the lines and pull a safe distance away before the *Ourang Medan* blew up and sank.

OFF THE DEEP END

Q: *What happens when you throw a red rock into the Black Sea?*

A: It sinks.

Q: *What happens when you throw a green rock into the Red Sea?*

A: It gets wet.

Mom: Did you give the goldfish fresh water today?

Kid: No, they haven't finished the water I gave them yesterday.

Q: *What do sea monsters eat?*

A: Fish and ships.

Q: *Where do ghosts swim in North America?*

A: In Lake Erie.

Q: *What do you get when you graduate from scuba diving school?*

A: A deep-loma.

GNARLY TEETH–
THE QUIZ!

Only one answer to each description is a real animal. The others are all phonies. Can you guess the real one?

1. This creature's nose is lined with long, pointed teeth. When it swims into a school of fish, it whips its snout around like a samurai sword, slashing fish left and right. If something good to eat is buried in the sand, it uses its nose like a rake to get at it.

a) Clam-rake shark   c) Spear shark

b) Sawshark   d) Samurai shark

2. It swims with its mouth slightly open, so it can breathe. On the hunt, it locks onto its target like a streamlined torpedo. This predator has 3,000 teeth in seven rows in its mouth. When a tooth breaks off, the one behind it moves forward and takes its place.

a) Torpedo shark   c) Great white shark

b) Mega-toothed shark   d) Sandpaper shark

3. This animal looks like it has a jousting lance attached to its head. The lance is actually a long, spiraled tooth. The animal is often seen floating on its back, its tusk pointing up at the sky. In medieval times, its tusks were sold as unicorn horns.

a) Unicorn whale   c) Spiraled-tusked whale

b) King Arthur's whale   d) Narwhal

Answers on next page. →

ANSWERS

1–b) The **sawshark** is actually a ray. Like other sharks and rays, it has special receptors on its snout that help it detect tiny electrical impulses of live

prey. It's not a danger to humans—unless you happen to get in the way of its nasty sharp nose.

2–c) The **great white shark**'s teeth are made for grab-

bing and tearing. But these teeth are more sensitive than your fingertips. That's why great white sharks "mouth" their prey first, to see if it's a tasty enough to eat. But the taste-test can be bad news for most animals: Even if the great white decides not to take a second bite, the "mouthing" is often fatal.

3–d) The **narwhal**'s mysterious tusk (its left front tooth, actually) is the only spiraled tusk in nature. And, unlike most teeth, it's soft on the outside and hard on the inside. It is so sensitive that the narwhal may be able to detect changes in weather —which is important when you live in the icy waters of the Arctic Ocean.

AMAZING JOURNEY

When Cassandra Villanueve boarded the ferryboat *Aloha* on June 2, 1974, she thought it would be just another ho-hum crossing between the Philippine islands. But 600 miles south of Manila, the *Aloha* caught fire and sank. In the confusion, Mrs. Villanueve fell overboard. She drifted in the rough seas for 12 hours (thankfully, she'd had time to put on a life jacket). When help arrived, it came in the form of a giant sea turtle! The turtle dove down and came up beneath Mrs. Villanueve, lifting her straight out of the water, and began to swim with her on its back. Soon a much smaller turtle climbed onto the turtle's back beside Mrs. Villanueve. It seems the little turtle had decided Mrs. Villanueve had to stay awake, because whenever she dozed off, it nipped her on the back. Two days later, a Philippine navy ship found them. When the sailors pulled Mrs. Villanueve onto a rescue boat, the sea turtles slipped beneath the waves and disappeared.

TURTLE TIMES

Fascinating facts about one of the world's great swimmers.

- Sea turtles have been swimming in the oceans since the time of the dinosaurs—around 75 million years.

- The *leatherback turtle* is the fastest swimmer. They've been timed at a speed of 22 miles per hour!

- Sea turtles have an excellent sense of time and direction. Scientists think they use the Earth's magnetic field to navigate thousands of miles across the ocean.

- Sea turtles can see very well under water, but out of the water their vision is blurry and nearsighted.

- Unlike land turtles, sea turtles cannot pull their heads and flippers into their shells for protection.

- When baby sea turtles first enter the water, a "swim frenzy" takes over. They will swim nonstop for 24 to 48 hours to get to deeper, safer water.

- Scientists call the first year of a baby sea turtle's life "the lost year" because they are rarely seen during that time.

- Of every 1,000 turtle eggs buried in the sand, only 800 will hatch. Of those 800, only 400 will survive the dangerous run to the ocean. Of those 400, only 200 will live for more than two years, and only *one* will survive the hazards of the sea to become an adult. That turtle can expect to live from 30 to 70 years.

- Once they enter the water, male sea turtles never

leave the sea. (Females return to the beach where they were born to lay their eggs.)

• Some turtles can actually breathe through their butts. All turtles have a hole between their back legs called a *cloaca* that they use to get rid of poop and pee, as well as lay their eggs. Some small turtles suck in air through their *cloaca* and save it in little air sacs. The Fitzroy River turtle of Australia gets almost two-thirds of its air this way.

MORE DOLPHIN FACTS

➤ Dolphins love to play. Favorite games? Blowing bubbles, tag, and toss-the-seaweed.

➤ Dolphins are closely related to cows, pigs, and deer.

➤ A dolphin's skin feels like rubber.

➤ A bottlenose dolphin replaces its top layer of skin every two hours.

➤ Dolphins can dive down 1,000 feet under the ocean and come right back up. If a human diver did that, the sudden change in water pressure would kill him.

➤ A dolphin can propel itself through the water at more than 24 mph. A human needs a boat to go that fast.

➤ Dolphins use *echolocation* to "see" in murky water. By listening to the echoes of their clicks, dolphins can identify the size and location of objects they can't see with their eyes.

THE LOST WORLD

People have been looking for the lost continent of Atlantis for 2,000 years—but did it ever really exist?

THE LEGEND

About 12,000 years ago, according to some stories, a great civilization called Atlantis sprang up on an island continent in the western ocean. The Atlanteans were light-years ahead of other humans, and their advanced technology made them the masters of the world. They built great temples and monuments in their dazzling city. Nothing seemed beyond the reach of their immense power. Then suddenly—they were gone. A violent earthquake ripped open a gaping hole in the ocean. Atlantis sank into the sea and was never seen again.

WHERE'D IT GO?

The Greek philosopher Plato first wrote about this mysterious lost world in 355 B.C. He even described the layout of the city in great detail, included its network of canals. Plato believed Atlantis was located west of the "Pillars of Hercules," the old name for the Strait of Gibraltar. That's the narrow channel that divides Spain from Morocco, and the Mediterranean Sea from the Atlantic Ocean. For centuries, explorers and historians thought the Azores, a series of lonely islands dotting a remote section of the Atlantic Ocean west of Gibraltar, were the remnants of the mountain peaks of Atlantis. But a geological survey of the ocean floor showed it to be covered with a thick layer of undisturbed mud that took millions of years to accumulate. There was no evidence of a sinking landmass or earthquake.

THE MINOAN SOLUTION

A history professor named K.T. Frost came up with a more likely candidate. The island of Crete lies only a few hundred miles south of the Greek mainland in the Aegean Sea. Centuries before Plato's time, it was home to the Minoans, a brilliant civilization that ruled the Mediterranean. Like the Atlanteans, the Minoans were more advanced than their Greek neighbors. They had great palaces filled with beautiful paintings. And like the Atlanteans, the Minoans vanished almost overnight.

A likely spot for the city of Atlantis can be found 10 miles off the coast of Crete on the small island of Santorini. Today Santorini is actually several little islands ringing a central lagoon, but 2,500 years ago it was one big island with a volcano at its center. In the year 1500 B.C.—900 years before Plato's time—that volcano exploded. The explosion caused a tidal wave 100 feet high, which swept over the sea and a mile inland, obliterating the great Minoan civilization in the same way Plato described the end of Atlantis.

THE SEARCH GOES ON

But some experts aren't satisfied with the Minoan theory, since Plato wrote that the fall of Atlantis occurred 9,000 years before his time, not 900. And he was adamant that the continent of Atlantis lay to the *west* of Greece, not to the south like Crete. So explorers continue to scour the oceans of the world for evidence of Atlantis. So far, no one has been able to provide convincing proof that Atlantis was ever more than a figment of Plato's imagination. But that hasn't stopped adventurers from trying. One theory suggests that the great city was indeed in the Atlantic Ocean, but much farther away, in the Bermuda Triangle off the coast of Florida. Others put the lost continent back in the Mediterranean, near the island of Cyprus, or in the North Atlantic, near Ireland. And the most extreme theory says that Atlantis was really on the *other* side of the world...in the South China Sea, off the coast of Vietnam.

FISH CAN FLY?

Not every fish in the sea is a swimmer.

FLYING FISH. The 50 species of flying fish around the world come in many colors and shapes, but they all have one thing in common—huge pectoral (chest) fins. These "wings" let flying fish escape predators by leaping out of the water and gliding for up to 350 feet! They can launch themselves into the air at 30 mph, too, which makes them difficult to catch. Unfortunately, they don't have much control over their landing, so flying fish often wind up stranded on the decks of boats.

MUDSKIPPERS. These little fish (1–3 inches) can't fly, but they can walk. They spend more of their lives out of the water than in it. In fact, they walk faster than they swim. Their pectoral fins work much like legs, which is great for fish that live in tidal areas where the water comes and goes unpredictably. Mudskippers have gills like regular fish, but they can also absorb oxygen right through their skin.

DON'T BITE ME!

The eel with sharp teeth and a bad rep.

Okay, first of all, the *moray eel* is not an eel. Or a sea snake. It's a fish. Two hundred species of morays live in tropical seas around the world. Sometimes they're called the *painted eel* because of the amazing variety of patterns and colors they have as camouflage. Some morays are polka-dotted; others are orange, bright yellow, or even zebra-striped. But unlike other fish, morays don't have scales—they have skin. It's thick and tough and covered with slime.

With its mouthful of sharp teeth, the moray eel looks really nasty. But it's actually a shy, docile creature. It can't see very well, so it would much rather spend its day holed up in a small rocky crevice than venture out in the open to bite off the toes of a nosy diver. So why do morays bare their teeth like they're snarling? They have to keep their mouths open to breathe. But be careful! If you bother one by sticking your hand near its hiding place, you may get a vicious bite. It's not because the moray eel's a meanie, though. It's because you just scared the slime out of it!

GODS OF THE SEA

Confronted with the awesome power of the ocean, ancient people believed there had to be a god behind it.

POSEIDON

Origin: Greece

Background: Poseidon lives in a beautiful palace in the kingdom of Atlantis. He's usually seen with a horse, carrying a three-pronged pitchfork known as a *trident*. It's a good idea not to upset Poseidon—he tends to cause earthquakes when he gets angry. (He's also the god of horses, rivers… and earthquakes.)

ÆGIR

Origin: Scandinavia

Background: Ægir is a giant, and he loves to party. His elaborate banquets are famous among the other Norse gods. Ægir has no problem sinking a boat, and carrying off its cargo and crew to his golden palace at the bottom of the sea. To stay on Ægir's good side, Viking sailors would kill a prisoner as a sacrifice before setting sail.

RYUJIN

Origin: Japan

Background: Ryujin owns the magical Tide Jewels

that control the tides and make tsunamis. He is the dragon god of the sea, but may also appear as a human being. In his huge red and white coral palace on the ocean bottom, human fish are his servants and sea turtles are his personal messengers. One day in Ryujin's palace is equal to 100 years on land.

KANALOA

Origin: Hawaii

Background: Also called the Great Octopus, Kanaloa is magician, a healer, and god of the underworld. He lives in a place known as the "lost islands" and is almost always seen with Kane, the god of the land and the trees, either fishing, sailing, or finding fresh water. Kanaloa always takes the shape of an octopus or squid. Hawaiian fishermen still look to him for protection.

MANANNAN MAC LIR

Origin: Ireland

Background: This god has a cloak of invisibility, and can forecast the weather. Manannan mac Lir is most often seen riding over the waves in his chariot, wearing a helmet of flames. He also owns a magical ship, the *Wave Sweeper*, which doesn't need wind or sails to speed across the ocean.

LEMANJA

Origin: Africa

Background: The Queen of the Sea, and protector of sailors and fishermen, Lemanja is not only beautiful, but compassionate, too. Anyone who dies at sea may live with her in her palace at the bottom of the sea. Sometimes she rises to the surface to listen to the songs sailors sing to her.

FREE WILLY

The star of three major motion pictures was an orca named Keiko.

Keiko was two years old when he was captured by a fisherman off the coast of Iceland and sold to a marine amusement park. Thus began his long career in show business: Keiko performed tricks in Iceland and Canada before he finally ended up at Reino Aventura, an amusement park in Mexico City. The public loved Keiko, but living in a cramped freshwater tank isn't good for an orca. In 1992 Keiko was discovered by Hollywood and starred in the movie *Free Willy*, about a boy who wanted to free a killer whale from a marine theme park. In a life-imitates-art moment, fans of the movie formed the Free Willy/Keiko Foundation to help Keiko escape his miserable life in Mexico City. He was airlifted first to Oregon, and then to Iceland where he swam in salt water and was taught how to hunt live fish like other orcas. When Keiko was finally released into the open waters, he swam 870 miles to the Taknes Fjord in Norway. He died at the ripe old age of 27, free at last.

WOOF! IT'S A WHALE

*The ancestor of today's whales
looked a lot like man's best friend.*

Whales are huge, have no legs, and live in the ocean, right? Well, that's true today, but 50 million years ago, the first whale actually looked more like a dog. It wasn't very big, either—about the size of a wolf. It didn't even live in the ocean. *Pakicetus* (its scientific name) hunted fish along the shores of the shallow seas that covered the Punjab region of Asia. Today the Punjab, which is in India and Pakistan, is almost a desert.

How do scientists know *pakicetus* was a whale? Because of the unusual structure of the ear region of its skull—a shape found only in whales, dolphins, and their ancestors.

THE LARGEST LIVING THING

It's over a thousand miles long...and it's ALIVE!

WHAT IS...

)● ...the largest living organism on the planet?

)● ...one of the Seven Natural Wonders of the World?

)● ...and something so big it can be seen from the International Space Station?

IF YOU GUESSED THE GREAT BARRIER REEF, YOU'RE RIGHT!

The Great Barrier Reef stretches for 1,616 miles off the northeast coast of Australia, and consists of more than 3,000 individual reefs and 900 islands.

(*Wait a minute*, you're thinking. *I thought you said it was alive.*)

It is. Although those islands and undersea reefs look and feel as hard as rock, they're actually made up of millions of tiny animals called coral *polyps*. These little creatures live in vast colonies in the tropical seas of the world. They build hard houses for themselves out of calcium carbonate. As they die, new polyps build new houses on top of the old ones. These polyps are very small, maybe the size of your fingernail, and only grow a few inches per year. But after 10,000 years, that makes for a lot of reef. In fact, it's the Great Barrier Reef—which is almost the same size as California, and the largest structure ever built by living things. (So much for the Empire State Building, the Pyramids, and the Great Wall of China!)

The Great Barrier Reef, seen from space.

It's also one of the richest habitats for marine life in the world. Over 1,500 species of fish call it home. So do 8,000 types of sponges, worms, shellfish, and crustaceans. There are 800 types of starfish and urchins alone. Humpback whales and dolphins breed there. Six of the seven species of sea turtle roam its lagoons. Poisonous sea snakes and jellyfish, too. Dugongs, the gentle cousins of the manatee, loll in its waters. And of course, there are always *lots* of sharks.

SLIMY SEA MOVIES

These movies will make you want to stay on land forever.

1. *The Poseidon Adventure* (1972)

A cruise ship gets flipped by a monster wave. Next time, take a plane to your vacation spot.

2. *The Abyss* (1989)

Aliens with attitude at the bottom of the ocean. What could be better?

3. *Titanic* (1997)

The biggest ship ever built runs into an iceberg. Bye-bye, *Titanic*!

4. *Waterworld* (1995)

The polar ice caps have melted and the entire globe is covered in water. A peek at the future after global warming?

5. *Jaws* (1975)

"Just when you thought it was safe to go back in the water..." Enough said.

6. *Creature from the Black Lagoon* (1954)

A mutant fish-man terrorizes the coast of Florida. Look close, and you can see the zipper on his costume when he swims by!

7. *The Incredible Mr. Limpet* (1964)

A nerdy human becomes a nerdy fish and saves the world. Yeah, right...

8. *Moby Dick* (1956)

Crazy Captain Ahab hunts the great white whale. Or is it the other way around?

9. *Deep Rising* (1998)

A monster squid attacks a cruise ship. Help!

10. *The Perfect Storm* (2000)

An itty-bitty fishing boat meets a monster wave. Guess who loses?

KILLER CLAMS...NOT!

A big mollusk with a bad reputation.

Giant clams are big. *Really* big. They can grow to the size of a beach umbrella and weigh over 500 pounds. They're so big that they were once thought to be maneaters—divers told tales of open clams snapping shut on unwary victims and not letting go. Old horror movies are full of scenes of killer clams chomping down scuba divers. The belief was so common that early versions of the U.S. Navy Diving Manual included instructions for escaping a giant clam's death-grip.

Actually, the giant clam is more dangerous out of the water than in: Most giant clam injuries occur when people drop the heavy shells on their toes. In reality, the giant clam closes its shell so slowly that you'd have to be sound asleep not to notice it shutting on you.

The strangest thing about the giant clam is that it's part animal and part plant. Like plants, it uses sunlight to make food. And just like many of the marine animals that share its home on the coral reef, the giant clam filters food from the ocean. With two ways of getting food, maybe that's why they grow so big. One thing's for certain, the giant clam is not a killer—unless of course, someone drops one on your head.

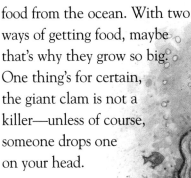

GLOBSTERS

What's shapeless, looks like goop, and really, really stinks?

A *globster* is a very weird, completely baffling object that might be found on any beach. Think of a big

pile of jelly-like, fatty flesh. There might be a huge tentacle or a strange-looking flipper sticking out of the goop. Sometimes it has hair, but it never has bones, scales, or cartilage. And the worst part: It stinks…a lot. Most globsters are eventually identified as the fatty remains of dead whales or giant squids. Some of the hardest to identify have turned out to be dead basking sharks, one of the largest (and strangest) fish in the ocean. But some globsters remain unidentified—a gooey, gross reminder that there are still unsolved mysteries in the deep.

SLIMY SEA FACT

Carolus Linnaeus, the great Swedish scientist who created the naming system we use to label of all living things, was a steadfast believer in sea monsters.

SEA ANIMAL QUIZ #2: BATHING BEAUTY?

1. It's the only marine mammal that can live in fresh or salt water, as long as the water is shallow and warm.

2. Its closest relatives are elephants, hyraxes (a rabbit-sized rodent from the Middle East), and aardvarks.

3. It has three to four fingernails on each of its flippers.

4. It has a mouthful of wide, flat teeth called "marching molars." It constantly replaces them, just like a shark—when one falls out, another moves forward.

5. It has a tail shaped like a paddle.

6. It knows how to have fun in the water. It can do headstands, tail stands, somersaults, barrel rolls—even bodysurf!

7. It farts a lot! That's because it only eats plants—as much as 110 pounds a day.

8. It sounds like a mouse, with squeaks, whistles, and chirps.

9. A grown member of this species can be as big as a pickup truck.

10. When European sailors first saw this creature, they thought it was a mermaid.

WHAT IS IT?

NINE AMAZING FISH FACTS

These may sound fishy, but Uncle John swears they are absolutely true.

1. **A lobster's teeth are in its stomach.**

2. **A shrimp's heart is in its head.**

3. **A horseshoe crab has 10 eyes.** They're placed all over its body—even on its tail.

4. **You can guess a fish's age by its scales.** You can count the growth rings, just like you'd count the rings on a tree.

5. **Fish can get seasick.** Keep a fish in a pail of water on a rolling ship, and sooner or later that fish will barf.

6. **Fish get dandruff.** Like humans, it's caused by flaking skin, and there's nothing they can do about it.

7. **Some fish can breathe air.** Small fish like *betas* and *gouramis* have an organ called a *labyrinth* that lets them breathe fresh air. It allows them to survive in water with low oxygen levels.

8. **Fish can talk to each other.** Some rasp their teeth or make noises in their throats; other fish use their swim bladders like a horn.

9. **Fish can change sex.** Boy? Girl? Many fish start out as one sex and turn into the other one later on. Some deepwater fish are both sexes all the time. Then they never need to look for a mate to have babies.

267

ESCAPE ARTIST

The legendary Houdini claimed he was the greatest escape artist who ever lived. But he might have met his match with the octopus.

What has eight arms, two eyes, and a beak? You guessed it. The octopus. It doesn't have a nose, ears, or fingers, but each arm is covered with a double row of white suction cups called

suckers. It uses these suckers to explore its world. Each sucker moves by itself like the way we wiggle our toes or fingers. And a sucker not only grips objects, it tastes them. An octopus has a beak like a bird, and a tongue—called a *radula*—that's covered with razor-sharp teeth. These teeth are able to cut through crab and snail shells like a buzzsaw. An octopus will often carry a crab back to its den for dinner. Then, after it's finished eating, the octopus will deposit the shells just outside its den. Very tidy!

The octopus is the great shape-shifter of the sea. It can make itself big and wide like an umbrella, or long and thin like a piece of rope. It can squeeze through cracks under a rock or flatten itself against the walls of a cave. The octopus is also a master of disguise. Its skin can change color instantly, acting as a camouflage to protect it from sharks and other predators.

When it comes to brains, the octopus goes to the head of the class. It is the smartest of all invertebrates. It can find its way through a maze, or figure out how to unscrew the lid of a jar and remove the tasty fish that's inside. The octopus is a very curious creature, and can actually die of boredom if kept in a tank with no world to explore and nothing to entertain it.

It can be pretty sneaky, too. Scientists at an aquarium were baffled by a mysterious disappearing act. Every day they'd place new fish in a tank, but when they returned in the morning, the fish would be gone. Finally they set up a video camera to see who was stealing the fish. They watched in amazement as an octopus in a tank across the room waited for the museum to close, then squeezed its way out of its tank, slid across the floor, slipped into the fish tank, and ate all the fish. Then it crawled back into its own tank and took a nap!

Caught in the act! This octopus is sneaking out of its tank through a tiny crack.

SCHOOLBOY SAILOR

Ever dream of going on an adventure? This teen did it.

Robin Lee Graham had just turned 16 when he asked his parents for a sail-boat. When they asked why, he said, "So I can sail around the world." He didn't even have a driver's license, yet in the summer of 1965 this high school student set sail from Los Angeles on an epic journey. On his tiny 24-foot-long boat, the *Dove*, he took a guitar, a radio, and two kittens for company. He made it to Hawaii…and decided to keep going. Most experienced sailors thought he'd never make it home. Sure, Robin had sailed a lot with his parents during his early teen years. He even knew how to navigate using the stars. But this was a giant trip and he was all alone. Still, Robin kept going.

He survived storms that swept him overboard and broke his mast. He was nearly mowed down by giant tanker ships. Once, he sat dead in the water for 22 days waiting for the wind to blow again. Yet somehow he was able to overcome every obstacle. In the Fiji Islands, he met and married a girl named Patti. But Robin was deter-mined to finish his solo voyage alone. When he finally sailed into the bay of Los Angeles, hundreds of boats came out to greet him. "By the end of my voyage," he said, "I had traveled over 33,000 miles. I was two inches taller and five years older. I was married and soon to be a father. I was a man—but I still couldn't drive a car!"

MERMAIDS

There's something fishy about this tale.

Their Japanese name is *ningyo*. In the Caribbean they're called *aycayia*. West Africans call them *mami wata*. Folk tales of half-human/half-fish creatures go as far back as 1000 BC. And most of these mythical sea folk are female—the *mermaids*.

Mermaids often have long hair, and sing haunting songs that drive sailors mad with longing. Some are said to be able to grant wishes or foretell the future, while others kidnap people and take them to their underwater kingdom. *Selkies* from Scotland, Ireland, and Iceland are rumored to be women who take the shape of seals, then shed their sealskins when they come on land to marry and have children.

But do they really exist? Christopher Columbus thought so. On his journey to the New World, he wrote in his journal that he and his crew spotted mermaids in the Caribbean Sea. He said he was surprised the mermaids were so ugly. (Historians suspect that what Columbus saw were actually manatees, which might resemble humans from a distance because they cradle their young in their arms.)

SPEED SHARK

*Ms. Jaws takes a holiday—and breaks
every speed record known to sharks.*

As great white sharks go, Nicole is not an exceptional specimen. She's only 12 feet long and weighs 3,000 pounds (the biggest great white on record was 23 feet long and weighed 7,000 pounds). But Nicole (named after Australian actress Nicole Kidman) recently did something no other shark has ever done before—she swam farther than any known shark ever swam before, and she did it faster. Nicole swam from South Africa to

Australia and back, a distance of 12,400 miles, and she covered the huge distance in only nine months.

The reason scientists know about Nicole's feat was that she had been tagged with a tracking sensor a few weeks before she embarked on her record-breaking swim. Scientists used to think great whites hung around coastal waters eating the

plentiful food that lived there, and didn't venture out into the open ocean. But recent research seems to indicate otherwise. Scientists were hoping that Nicole's sensor would provide them with some clues as to where the sharks went, and why.

Their best guess is that Nicole was husband-hunting, since she had lots of food in South Africa year round and had no reason to look for it elsewhere. But what surprised the scientists was how Nicole swam straight as an arrow across the ocean. Although she dove frequently, sometimes as deep as 3,000 feet, Nicole spent more than half her swim time right at the surface. Shark researcher Ramon Bonfil thinks Nicole was using the stars and moon to find her way to Australia, and back again.

So, did Nicole find a boyfriend on her trip to Australia? If she did, she's not telling.

THE SLIMY "SEE"

B rian Reel and the folks at Aqua One Technologies were sitting on this idea for a long time. Now you can sit on it, too. It's the Fish n' Flush, the only toilet in the world with a built-in aquarium.

Brian adds that if you don't like fish, you can make it into a terrarium and put other animals in there—like lizards, snakes, and scorpions.

Uncle John's

STRANGE & SCARY

Freaky Facts about Peculiar People

BATHROOM READER
FOR KIDS ONLY!

by the **Bathroom Readers' Institute**

Tales from the BARK side

Boo!
Don't be scared—it's only
me, Porter the Wonder Dog.
I'm wearing this disguise
because Uncle John told me
that ghosts can't get me if they
can't recognize me (although I
suspect his real reason was to
trick me into wearing these dorky glasses).

Before you start reading, you might want to get
your own disguise. Because I warn you: There are
a lot of strange characters roaming through these
pages—ghosts, vampires, zombies, aliens, a lizard
guy, a real wolf-man…and a guy who wears inflatable underwear.

Here's Part Three of *Creature Feature:*

Strange & Scary!

CABBAGE PATCH SON

And you think your family's weird!

Pat and Joe Prosey from Leonardtown, Maryland, have spent 19 years raising a Cabbage Patch doll as their only son. Kevin, as they call him, is a one-foot-tall doll, "adopted" from the Coleco toy company. "With every kid that you adopt, you promise to love them and be a good parent, and take care of this child," Pat Prosey explained. "And that's what we did with Kevin."

Their Cabbage Patch son has his own playroom, a complete wardrobe, his own pet dog, and a bright red (doll-sized) Corvette for zipping around the driveway. They've even set up a college fund for him.

The couple takes Kevin on all of their vacations. When they talk to the doll, he answers back—in a voice supplied by Joe.

The Proseys actually have a real daughter, too (her name is Vicky), but they've told reporters that Kevin is the ideal child. "He's easygoing, quiet, and well-behaved."

GAG ME WITH A SNEAKER

To find success, sometimes you must meet with de-feet.

It's official! Noah Nielsen has America's smelliest sneakers. Odor Eaters, maker of anti-foot odor products, declared Noah the winner in their 30th annual competition. Contestants came from as far away as Alaska, Texas, Washington, Arkansas, and Utah to compete, but the 10-year-old from Vermont was the winner.

Noah credits his success to "No socks, ever!" His sweaty, dirt-encrusted toes—which can be seen through the gaping holes in his Adidas—are the reason his shoes are so ripe. In fact, Noah's feet were so foul that during the competition one judge gagged and another staggered backward, crying, "Human feet shouldn't smell that bad!" But Noah just smiled because he won a $500 savings bond, a $100 check for new sneakers, and a large supply of Odor Eaters. P-U!

IF THE SHOE FITS

FEET FACTS

• Presidents George Washington, Abraham Lincoln, and Bill Clinton all wore size 13 shoes.

• Your feet can be up to 10 percent larger by the end of the day.

• What do you do when you need a little luck? According to Irish folklore, just nail a shoe to a tree. In 1996 a property owner in Bainbridge, Ohio, nailed a shoe to his tree for luck. Before he knew it shoes of all shapes and sizes were nailed next to his. Now the tree is known far and wide as…the Shoe Tree.

BUSTED!

Charles Taylor of Wichita, Kansas, was charged with holding up a store and stealing a pair of boots worth $70. At his trial, the man pleaded "not guilty," and then took the witness stand wearing the stolen boots…with the tags still on them! (The jury found him guilty.)

MONSTER LINEUP

Thousands of people claim to have seen these creatures. Have you? Here's the scoop on America's least wanted.

MOTHMAN

Description: Stands seven feet tall. Has no head, yet has bright red eyes on top of its shoulders. Flies with featherless wings.

Behavior: Mothman screeches loudly and flies at speeds of up to 100 mph, sometimes straight up in the air like a rocket. Dogs disappear and UFOs are often sighted after an appearance.

Last Seen: Point Pleasant, West Virginia

BIGFOOT

Description: Seven to eight feet tall, weighs 300 pounds. Has reddish brown fur, long arms, and big humanlike feet.

Behavior: Bigfoot smells really bad, like a cross between a skunk and a wet dog. He is very shy so he runs away from humans, but he often leaves a strange calling card of stick structures woven into the forks of trees.

Last Seen: Lots of places, such as Northern California, Oregon, Washington, British Columbia, and Texas.

ZOMBIE

Profile: The "walking dead." Has a blank face and staggering walk and speaks very slowly.

Behavior: Zombies are corpses raised from the grave by voodoo sorcerers, or *bokors*. They become mindless slaves seeking revenge for the bokor. Only a taste of salt will release the zombie so it can return to its grave.

Last Seen: Haiti

THE JERSEY DEVIL

Description: A cross between a snake, a horse, and a bird. And it flies.

Behavior: The Jersey Devil has terrorized the Pine Barrens of New Jersey for more than 260 years. It has been seen by more than 2,000 witnesses. A terrible disaster often follows this creature's appearance.

Last Seen: New Jersey (obviously).

TOY STORIES

Here's what happens when toy makers go...weird.

THUGGIES. These dolls come with something that no dolls ever had before—criminal records. That's right, "Motorcycle Meanie," "Dickie the Dealer," and "Bonnie Ann Bribe" are all crooks who come packaged in their own jail cells. Introduced in 1993, Thuggies were designed to teach kids that crime doesn't pay.

FORWARD COMMAND POST. Grandma's dollhouse never looked like this. Imagine a two-story house that's been taken over by soldiers in a war zone, and you've got Ever Sparkle Toys' strange creation. This bombed-out dollhouse comes with broken railings, walls filled

with bullet holes, and soldiers armed with long-range sniper rifles. This 75-piece set includes high-tech cannons, weapons in footlockers, explosives, camo combat gear, and an American flag. (Ages 5 and up.)

WHAT'S IN NED'S HEAD?

Ned's Head is a stuffed plush head filled with gross plastic things—fake vomit, moldy cheese, rats, spiders, worms, and more. Kids compete by fishing the yucky  stuff out of Ed's ears, nose, and mouth. The award-winning game's creators call Ned's Head "a wacky, silly, icky, sticky, and fun gross-out game." It is.

SECRET AGENT DOLL

The National Security Agency banned Furbys from their headquarters because these fuzzy toys have embedded computer chips that allow them to record and repeat what they "hear." Officials were afraid they might remember phrases that are **TOP SECRET**.

FEAR FACTOR

Check out these famous fraidy cats.

QUEEN ELIZABETH I. England's most famous queen had a fear of roses.

THOMAS EDISON. The inventor of the lightbulb was afraid of the dark.

ELVIS PRESLEY. As a young boy, the "king of rock 'n' roll" carried his own fork and knife to school. Why? His mother thought germs on the cafeteria's silverware would make him sick.

NIKOLA TESLA. One of the world's greatest inventors was deathly afraid of round objects—especially pearl necklaces.

MOZART. When he was little, this famous composer was so scared of trumpets that he would get physically ill when he heard one blow.

RAY BRADBURY. He writes of traveling to distant planets, but this famous sci-fi author is actually afraid to fly.

YOU'RE MY INSPIRATION

Strange beginnings for strange characters.

OSCAR THE GROUCH

Muppets creator Jim Henson and *Sesame Street* director Jon Stone always had lunch at a New York restaurant called Oscar's Tavern. Their waiter was the rudest, grouchiest man they'd ever met. But they thought he was funny… so funny that they used him as the model for Oscar, the world's most famous grouch.

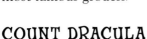

COUNT DRACULA

The inspiration for this batty villain was Prince Vlad, a 15th century Romanian ruler who had a nasty habit of impaling his enemies on sharp stakes (and dipping his bread in their blood). Vlad the Impaler, as he was known to his enemies, was also called Dracula, or "son of the dragon."

FREDDY KRUEGER

Writer/director Wes Craven based the evil character in his *Nightmare on Elm Street* films after a kid named Freddy who harassed and bullied him in high school.

REVOLTING RECORDS

FARTHEST NOSE BLOW
On August 13, 1999, Scot Jeckel launched a marshmallow from his nostril into the mouth of his friend Ray Perisin. The record blow: a mighty 16 feet, 3½ inches.

MOST COBRA KISSES
In 1999 Gordon Cates of Alachua, Florida, set a world record by kissing 11 deadly cobras in a row.

LOUDEST BURP
On April 5, 2000, Paul Hunn of London, England, burped one that registered 118.1 decibels. (That's almost as loud as a jumbo jet taking off.)

BIGGEST EYEBALL POPPER
Kim Goodman of Chicago set a strange world record on June 13, 1998, when she popped her eyeballs 11 millimeters (almost ½-inch) out of their sockets.

FARTHEST CRICKET SPITTER
The world record for farthest dead cricket spitting is 32 feet. It was set in 1998 by Dan Capps at Purdue University's annual Bug Bowl in West Lafayette, Indiana.

FASTEST WORM EATER

On November 15, 2003, "Snake" Manoharan of Madras, India, ate 200 earthworms in 30 seconds, breaking the previous record set by American Mike Hogg. (Snake likes to finish off his worm-eating act by putting his pet snake up his nose and pulling it out through his mouth.)

FARTHEST MILK SQUIRT

Ilker Yilmaz has an unusual talent. He can squirt milk from his eye. And he squirts it farther than anyone else in the world. He proved it on September 1, 2004, when he shot some milk 9 feet 2 inches at the Armada Hotel in Istanbul, Turkey.

MOST TIME SPENT WITH SCORPIONS

Nur Malena Hassan from Malaysia set a world record in 2004. Her feat: she endured 36 days locked in a small glass box with 6,069 scorpions. The 27-year-old Scorpion Queen was stung 17 times…and lived to tell about it!

CREEPY CURES

Don't try these at home, but before modern medicine, people relied on folk remedies. How, for example, would they cure...

A TOOTHACHE?
Chew on a peppercorn.

SWOLLEN EYES?
Take a live crab; remove its eyes. Put the crab back in the water and put the eyeballs on your neck.

SORE THROAT? Tie
nine knots in a black thread and wear it around your neck for nine days.

SNAKEBITE? Put
earwax on the bite and ask someone to say a prayer for you.

INGROWN TOE-NAIL? Using a leather
string, tie a lizard's liver to your left ankle. The ingrown nail should disappear in nine days.

SHORTNESS OF BREATH? Take the
lungs and liver from a fox. Chop them up into tiny pieces, mix with wine, and drink the concoction from a church bell.

BURNS? Mix sheep
dung with fresh goose grease and spread it on the affected area.

FRECKLES? Four-
day-old lemon juice rubbed on the face will make them go away.

CUTS? Apply a large
army ant to the cut, so that it takes hold of each side of the wound with its pincers. Cut the body off, leaving the ant's head to hold the cut together.

HIDE AND SEEK?

*World War II ended in 1945...but
somebody forgot to tell this guy.*

Lieutenant Hiroo Onoda of the Imperial Japanese
Army survived in the jungles of the tiny Philippine
island of Lubang for nearly three decades by hunting in
the forests and stealing food from villagers. Then on February 20, 1974, Onoda met a young Japanese adventurer
named Norio Suzuki, who had come to the Philippines to
search for him. The two became friends, and Suzuki
explained to the old warrior that the fighting had stopped
a long time ago. Yet when he asked Onoda to return to
Japan, Onoda said he would not leave his post without
direct orders from one of his commanders. On March 9,
1974, Norio Suzuki brought Onoda's
onetime superior commander,
Major Taniguchi,
who delivered
the orders for
Onoda
to surrender.

BODY BY YOU

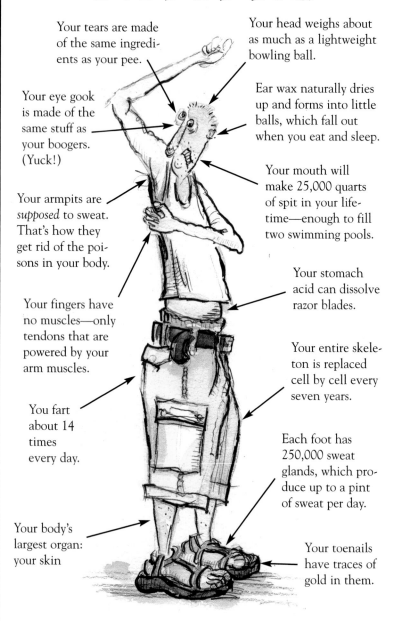

Your tears are made of the same ingredients as your pee.

Your head weighs about as much as a lightweight bowling ball.

Your eye gook is made of the same stuff as your boogers. (Yuck!)

Ear wax naturally dries up and forms into little balls, which fall out when you eat and sleep.

Your armpits are *supposed* to sweat. That's how they get rid of the poisons in your body.

Your mouth will make 25,000 quarts of spit in your lifetime—enough to fill two swimming pools.

Your fingers have no muscles—only tendons that are powered by your arm muscles.

Your stomach acid can dissolve razor blades.

Your entire skeleton is replaced cell by cell every seven years.

You fart about 14 times every day.

Each foot has 250,000 sweat glands, which produce up to a pint of sweat per day.

Your body's largest organ: your skin

Your toenails have traces of gold in them.

EW! GROSS!

BOMBS AWAY!

Joe Carlone and his wife spent 12 years trying to rid their house of a terrible smell, but nothing seemed to help. Then one day their kitchen wall burst and 40 gallons of sewage gushed into the room. Years before, a telephone installer had accidentally punctured a pipe coming from the upstairs bathroom. The walls became so packed with poop they exploded.

NAVEL JELLY

Most people wash out their belly button lint, but not Graham Barker. He's been collecting his for more than 20 years, earning him a Guinness world record: "Most Belly Button Lint." When he gets enough fluff, he plans on stuffing a pillow with it.

Navel Fluff 1984–1993

Navel Fluff 1994 – 2000

Navel Fluff 2001 –

WHO DEALT IT SMELT IT

What is the world's stinkiest substance? It's a tie between "The U.S. Government Standard Bathroom Malodor" and "Who Me?" Both are used by the military in stink bombs, as a way to break up riots. One reeks of rotting food and sulfur; the other smells like human poop.

WEIRD UNDERWEAR

Boxers, briefs...or these?

INFLATABLE UNDERPANTS

Katsuo Katugoru of Tokyo, Japan, was so afraid of drowning that he invented something to protect him in case of emergency: inflatable underpants. Unfortunately, his underwear accidentally inflated while he was on the subway, instantly expanding to 30 times their normal size and nearly suffocating his seatmates. Luckily, some quick-thinking passengers burst his bubble—saving the day by stabbing the undies with pens and pencils.

WOLF MAN

Only 50 cases of this rare genetic condition have been documented since the Middle Ages. Could it be the root of wolf man legends around the world?

Jesus Fajardo Aceves is truly one-of-a-kind. Or rather, one-of-a-family. Twenty-four members of the Aceves family in Zacatecas, Mexico, have *hypertrichosis*, a genetic disorder that makes hair grow all over a person's body, including his face.

Very little is known about the condition because it shows up in only one out of ten million people. Some scientists believe "the curse of the hair" is caused by a holdover gene from the distant past, when humans were as hairy as apes.

What we do know is that throughout history, people with hypertrichosis have suffered terribly. They've been treated as freaks, put on display in circuses, or even worse, feared as monsters. But the truth is that "wolf people," as the Aceves family proudly call themselves, are completely normal...except for their hair!

WHIZ KIDS

Here are three stories of uniquely gifted kids.

MICHAEL KEARNEY (b. 1984) started talking when he was four months old. Two months later, baby Michael surprised his family again. He wasn't feeling well, so his mother took him to the doctor. That's when he told the doctor, "I have a left ear infection." When Michael was ten months old, his dad asked his mom, "Why don't we go out and get some F-R-E-N-C-H F-R-I-E-S?" "That sounds good," Michael piped up. "Let's go to M-C-D-O-N-A-L-D-S."

Michael entered high school at the age of five and finished nine months later. He was 10 when he graduated from college, and broke a Guinness world record at 14 by graduating from Middle Tennessee State University with a masters degree in chemistry.

JAY GREENBERG (b. 1991) likes to be called Blue Jay because, like Jay, a blue jay is small and makes lots of noise. But Jay doesn't exactly make noise—he composes orchestral music.

At two years old Jay started drawing musical instruments. One day he drew a cello and told his parents he wanted one. When his mother finally took him to a music store, Jay sat down at a miniature cello and immediately began to play, beautifully.

Jay started composing music the following year, when he was just three. Jay uses a computer program to write music, sometimes writing so fast that his computer crashes. In a field where talented composers might write five or six symphonies in their entire lifetime, Jay already composed five symphonies... before the age of 13.

GREGORY R. SMITH (b. 1989) learned how to read when he was two years old. He became a vegetarian that same year when he noticed that humans, like the herbivore dinosaurs he was studying, have flat teeth. Greg graduated from high school at 10 and earned a college degree in mathematics when he was 13.

He now works promoting nonviolence and world peace through the organization he founded, International Youth Advocates. And he's been nominated for the Nobel Peace Prize three times (he was just 12 years old when he was first nominated).

DOUBLE TROUBLE

Are twins more connected than normal siblings?

OH, BROTHER!

Identical twins from Piqua, Ohio, were adopted by families from different towns. The twins met again at age 39 and discovered

some remarkable facts: Both were named James. Each had married and divorced a woman named Linda, then married a woman named Betty. One's son was named James Alan; the other's was James Allen. Both did well in math and liked woodworking and drove the same model car and both had dogs named Toy. The biggest difference? James Lewis had short hair combed back; James Springer had long hair combed forward.

OH, SISTER!

In 1948 Diane Lamb broke two ribs in a train crash. At that exact moment her twin sister, who lived in another town, felt a stabbing pain in her chest, fell out of her chair, and broke the same two ribs.

OUCH! OUCH!

Roberto and Marco were identical twins who made a parachute jump together near Milan, Italy. Roberto broke his leg on landing. Two hours later Marco crashed his car while driving home...and broke *his* leg.

LUCKY FINDS #1

Keep your eyes open—you never know
when luck might be on your side.

THE FIND: A diamond

WHERE: Under a yam

THE STORY: In 1997 three orphan boys from Sierra Leone, Africa, were scrounging for food. They had already gone hungry for two days when, after a luckless morning of searching for yams near the village of Hinnah Malen, the starving boys gave up and decided to walk home. While walking along the road, they spotted a yam under a palm tree. As the boys pried the yam out of the ground, they discovered a flawless 100-carat diamond worth half a million dollars.

"86 THE BUNPUPS"

That's restaurant lingo for, "We're out of hot dogs." Here are some more:

"ADAM AND EVE ON A RAFT"
Two poached eggs on toast

"AN M.D."
A Dr Pepper

"BOSSY IN A BOWL"
Beef stew

"WAX"
American cheese

"HOUSE-BOAT"
A banana split

"MIKE AND IKE"
Salt and pepper shakers

"PUT A HAT ON IT"
Add ice cream

"LIFE PRESERVERS"
Doughnuts

"COW PASTE"
Butter

"NERVOUS PUDDING"
Jell-o

"PAINT A BOW-WOW RED"
A hot dog with ketchup

"HOLD THE HAIL"
No ice

"THROW IT IN THE MUD"
Add chocolate syrup

LOST AND FOUND

There are no "finders keepers, losers weepers" here.

LOST: A bus ticket

FOUND: Jack Crackers of Derbyshire, England, lost a bus ticket when he was just a teenager. Years later, at age 75, he was slapped on the back during a coughing fit and it fell out of his ear. Crackers got his ticket back and also his hearing— he'd been deaf in that ear for 60 years!

LOST: A wedding ring

FOUND: Mrs. Gudebrod of California lost her wedding ring during a picnic at a beach. A year later her husband brought home a crab he'd caught on the same beach. Guess what they found stuck to one of the crab's claws? Mrs. G's wedding ring.

WARNING!

Ever been warned not to do something stupid—so stupid that you would never even consider doing it? Here are some real labels found on real products.

On a Batman costume

"WARNING: CAPE DOES NOT ENABLE USER TO FLY."

On a toilet brush

"CAUTION: DO NOT USE FOR PERSONAL HYGIENE."

On a household iron

"WARNING: NEVER IRON CLOTHES WHILE THEY ARE BEING WORN."

On a washing machine

"CAUTION: YOU MUST REMOVE CLOTHES BEFORE WASHING"

On a king-size mattress

"WARNING: DO NOT ATTEMPT TO SWALLOW."

NATURE IS STRANGE

Weird facts from the natural world.

- Elephants are the only mammals that can't jump.

- Hummingbirds can't walk.

- Bees kill more people than snakes do.

- A rat can go longer without water than a camel.

- Possums don't actually "play" dead. They pass out from fear…and *look* dead.

- Only the female mosquito bites.

- A pregnant goldfish is called a *twit*.

- Crickets hear through their knees; butterflies taste with their feet.

- Snakes can see through their eyelids.

- Kangaroos can't jump backward.

- Mosquitoes prefer children to adults and blondes to brunettes.

- The venom of a female black widow spider is more potent than that of a rattlesnake.

- The praying mantis is the only insect that can rotate its head 360 degrees.

- More than 10,000 birds a year die from smashing into windows!

KING TUT'S CURSE

Who believes in curses? We do.

On November 26, 1922, a team led by a British archaeologist named Howard Carter entered the ancient Egyptian tomb of King Tutankhamen. Within seven years of that date, 11 of the 13 Europeans who were present when the tomb was opened were dead. Some believe a fungus found growing on the tomb's walls killed the explorers. Others believe the tomb was cursed.

What do *you* think?

THE FACTS

- On the day King Tut's tomb was opened, a vulture circled overhead. The archaeologists thought this was particularly strange. Why? Because according to legend, the tomb was guarded by Nekhbet, the vulture goddess. Her curse was printed above the door.

- Three months later, Lord Carnarvon, who had financed the expedition, was the first to go. He died crying, "There's a bird...scratching my face!" At the exact moment he passed away, the lights went out in Cairo and his dog at home in England howled in anguish...and then dropped dead.

- That same year Richard Bethell, Howard Carter's secretary, died of heart failure.

- A short time later, Arthur Mace, one of the archaeologists in the group who opened the tomb, fell into a coma. He died in 1923.

- Hugh Evelyn-White, another archaeologist with the expedition, hung himself in 1924. He left a note that read: "I have succumbed to a curse which forces me to disappear."

- The year the tomb was opened, a worker stole a piece of King Tut's jewelry. A relative of the thief returned it to the authorities 83 years later. Why? The curse. From the time the relative received the jewel, four untimely deaths had struck her family.

HOW TO MAKE
A MUMMY

An ancient secret recipe.

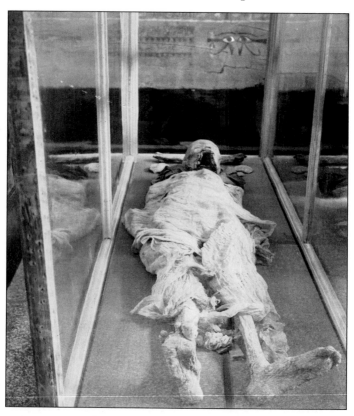

INGREDIENTS:
- 1 dead body
- 1 crochet hook
- several jars
- 400 pounds of salt
- frankincense
- myrrh
- lots of linen
- a small amulet

STEP ONE:

1. Using the crochet hook, pull the brains out through the nose.

2. Make a small incision in the belly and take out everything except the heart.

3. Place all the entrails (the stuff you pulled out) in the jars.

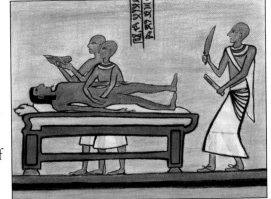

4. Stuff packets of salt inside the body, then completely cover the outside of the body with the rest of the salt.

5. Wait at least 35 days for the body to dry out and become mummified.

STEP TWO:

1. Carefully remove the salt.

2. Gently anoint the body with frankincense and myrrh (two ancient types of fragrant tree resin).

3. Wrap the body in layer after layer of linen strips.

4. During the wrapping procedure, place the small amulet over the heart. Decorate each layer with hiero-glyphic prayers.

STEP THREE:

For the total effect, let mummy rest undisturbed for at least a thousand years.

SLEEPING BEAUTY

The true tale of a real-life Rip Van Winkle.

On February 3, 1866, Mollie Fancher, a 23-year-old Brooklyn woman, felt dizzy and collapsed on the floor in a faint. Her aunt put her to bed, thinking Mollie would come out of it. But she didn't.

For the next 46 years, Mollie lay in a trance, barely breathing, eating, or drinking. Doctors were baffled. None knew what had caused this strange sleep, nor what to do about it. Then, nine years into her trance-like state, Mollie began to display amazing powers. She could describe the dress and actions of people hundreds of miles away, and could read unopened letters.

One famous test of her powers involved sealing a secret message inside three envelopes and then hiding it in her doctor's office five miles away. When the doctor asked Mollie what was in the envelope, she whispered, "Written on a sheet of paper are the words, 'Lincoln was shot by a crazed actor.'" She was right.

Mollie Fancher became known as the "Brooklyn Enigma" (an enigma is something mysterious and hard to understand). Then one day in 1912, the 70-year-old woman woke up. She lived three more years, but she remains an enigma. To this day, no one has ever fully explained what caused her long, strange sleep.

NEVERMORE

Every year on the nineteenth of January, a mysterious man sneaks into a locked graveyard in Baltimore, Maryland, and places three roses and a half-empty bottle of cognac on Edgar Allan Poe's grave. Poe, author of dark poems and stories like "The Raven" and "The Telltale Heart," died in 1849.

Jeff Jerome, curator of the Poe House and Museum, says the man first appeared in 1949. In 1993 the mystery mourner, who always wore a scarf and black hat, left a note that read, "The torch will be passed."

In 1999, the fifty-first year, a new mourner appeared.

This one followed the same ritual as the previous mystery man, placing the roses and cognac bottle on Poe's grave. He put his hand on top of the tombstone and bowed his head for five minutes. And then he disappeared... into the fog.

SPOOKY SPOTS

*Want to see a ghost? Visit scary Olde England—
there are plenty of ghosts for everyone.*

BORLEY RECTORY IN ESSEX

According to local legend, in the 17th century, a woman named Marie Laire was strangled by her husband and buried in the cellar of a monastery. Two hundred years later, Reverend Henry Bull unknowingly built Borley Rectory on the site where the monastery once stood. Marie Laire soon made her presence known. She often appeared at Reverend Bull's window, staring at him with vacant eyes. Bull was so upset that he bricked up the window...but the ghostly legend grew:

• In 1923, new owners called in a psychic investigator, who witnessed vases flying into walls, keys leaping from their keyholes, and messages being tapped out on a mirror.

• When the Reverend Lionel Foyster moved into the rectory, messages began to appear on the walls asking Foyster's wife, Marianne, to "please get help."

• In 1939 a mysterious fire destroyed the house. Some local residents claimed to have seen a nun at an upper window peering out over the flames.

THE INDUSTRIAL MUSEUM IN DERBY. Built on the site of an old silk mill, the museum's tower is haunted by the ghost of a little boy who worked at the factory and died when he was kicked down the stairs by one of the bosses. The staff often hear crying and run into the tower thinking there's a lost child inside. But it's always empty. Instead they find the elevator going up and down... by itself.

THE THEATRE ROYAL AT MARGATE. This theater doesn't need to put on scary shows—it's scary enough as it is. Many actors say they've heard a scream and seen an orange ball of light traveling across the stage before exiting through the stage door. An apparition sometimes appears in a box in the balcony and draws back the curtains if they are closed.

THE CROWN HOTEL IN YORKSHIRE. This 17th-century inn is now a three-star hotel that hosts a number of ghostly guests. The most famous: a waitress who was murdered by the chef and now wanders the corridors crying. A lady in a gown has been spotted in the lobby, where temperatures suddenly drop dramatically. One permanent resident of the hotel is often awakened by the ghost of a little girl sitting on her bed, and the ghost of the notorious highway robber Dick Turpin is heard galloping by outside.

TOMBSTONE TALES

If you're ever in Ohio, stop by and say AHHH!

GREAT BALL OF MYSTERY

Marion Cemetery in Marion, Ohio, is home to the "Merchant Ball." This 5,200-pound granite ball—the gravestone for the Charles Merchant family—rests solidly on a stone pedestal, but ever since 1898 it has rotated...all by itself. The family first noticed the phenomenon when a spot where the granite had not been polished suddenly

appeared. They tried to stop the ball from spinning. They had a crane lift the 2½-ton stone and tar it back into place. But it continued to turn!

What causes the mystery movement? Some say a restless spirit moves the ball. Others think it's a result of temperature changes, which make the base expand and contract. But that would leave scratches in the ball—there aren't any. It seems to float on its pedestal.

There are other stone balls in the Marion Cemetery, but they don't turn. The Merchant Ball remains an unsolved mystery.

ASHES TO ASHES?

Not everyone wants to end up six feet under. Edward Headrick, who invented the Frisbee, wanted his ashes molded into a Frisbee and tossed around. Here are some more ash-tonishing endings.

ASHES TO DIAMONDS. LifeGem Memorials turns dead people's remains into diamonds. The concept is simple. Humans and diamonds are both made up of carbon. Add pressure and heat and you've got a gem that will last forever. What's more, the average person's ashes contain enough carbon to make 50 to 100 beautiful diamonds.

ASHES TO ART. Wayne Gilbert, an artist from Texas, has made the amazing (and gruesome) discovery that every person has a unique color—even after death. He found this out when he mixed a person's ashes with resin…and color suddenly appeared. Now he turns people into paintings.

ASHES TO REEFS. Want to spend eternity with fish? Eternal Reefs mixes the ashes of deceased people with cement to create balls that are dropped into the ocean to create artificial reefs. The fish love the reefs.

ASHES TO SPACE DUST. A company called Celestis will launch the ashes of your loved one into deep space. "Families can look up into the night sky and know their loved ones are up there somewhere."

GHOST HUNTER

Who you gonna call? Nancy, of course.

In the 1970s, Professor Nancy Acuff was driving home from her job at East Tennessee University when she hit what she later called a "time warp." Suddenly she was transported back in time to the 1800s. Her home was gone and in its place stood a log cabin. She watched a man on horseback gallop up to the cabin door and yell for someone to come out. When a young boy appeared, the rider whirled around and galloped back down the road. Then, just as suddenly, everything changed back to the 1970s.

When a similar incident occurred a year later, Acuff did some investigating and concluded that the "man" was her home's previous owner, Jacob Storm, the first mayor of Blountville, Tennessee. Word of Professor Acuff's ghost hunting spread and soon she was getting calls from people with haunted homes of their own.

Acuff believes there is a difference between spirits and ghosts. Ghosts always do the same thing at the same location, but spirits are generally the souls of dead relatives who have some message or warning they want to impart. And Professor Acuff is there to receive it.

BAD GHOSTS!

Go on, spend the night here—we dare you.

The Ancient Ram Inn is an 800-year-old inn built on a pagan burial site in England. What scares most visitors is the creepy feeling that the spirits here are not friendly. John Humphries, who has lived there for 30 years, says he has been pushed against walls, knocked over, and had his bed shaken. Once he even felt something clawing at his bed like an animal.

But it is the Bishop's Room that frightens most people away. According to Julie Hunt, a well-known ghost hunter, the room is home to five phantoms, including a cavalier, a monk, and a witch.

In 1999 she took this photograph of a blurry figure in the room, which she believes is conclusive evidence of ghostly activity in the Ancient Ram Inn.

TA MOKO

The Maoris—the native people of New Zealand—were legendary warriors of the South Pacific. Ta moko is Maori for "to be tattooed." They awed their enemies with their amazing tattoos.

WHO GOT *TA MOKO*

All high-ranking Maori were tattooed as a rite of passage into adulthood. When young men and women reached age 12 or 13, girls tattooed their chins and boys got a full-face tattoo. The tattoos told not only a person's social status but also what tribe and clan he came from—even what he did for a living. The designs were so unique that during the 18th century, Maori men would sign legal documents by pressing their faces against the paper like a signature. Most young Maoris tattooed only their faces but they often added tattoos to

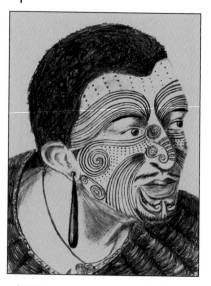

other parts of their bodies to mark important events in their lives. North Auckland warriors were famous for the double spirals tattooed from their butts to their knees. *Ta moko* was an incredibly painful ordeal that could last for days. But everyone tried to get through it. Why? Because not to have moko made you a real loser in Maori society.

HOW *TA MOKO* WAS DONE

The ta moko artist would study a young Maori's face for hours, even days, working out a design. Then he carved deep cuts into the skin with a bone chisel. Only the Maori did tattoos in this way (other Polynesians like the Samoans and Hawaiians used needles, which is the way most tattoos are made today). Next he dipped the chisel into a mixture of burned *kauri* tree gum and caterpillars and tapped the sooty powder into the grooves in the skin.

"OW! THAT HURTS!"

The pain a young Maori endured was so intense that friends and relatives would play flutes and chant poems to keep his mind off it. Sometimes the Maori would pass out or, even worse, quit, which shamed him for life. But getting the tattoo was just the first part of the ordeal. Once the tattoo artist was finished, leaves from the *karaka* tree were put on the cuts to help them heal, and that process took months. Nothing was allowed to touch the swollen wounds, which could get infected, so the Maori was fed liquid food and water through a wooden funnel. Depending on where the tattoos had been placed, he might not be able to get up and move around. But six months later the young Maori was usually fit enough to walk proudly out among his or her people with a totally new look.

THE AMITYVILLE HORROR

This story was the subject of a best-selling book and a very creepy movie. Is it truth...or fiction?

On November 13, 1974, six members of the DeFeo family were murdered by their oldest son, Ronald, in their home in Amityville, New York. One year later, George and Cathy Lutz and their three children moved into that home. Twenty-eight days later, the Lutz family moved out. Here are the reasons why.

Father Ray Pecoraro was brought in to bless the house. When he did, he felt an unseen hand slap him and heard a voice say, "Get out."

Black goo oozed out of keyholes in the doors.

Terrible odors filled the house.

The family heard weird music, like a brass band tuning up before playing.

The Lutz family heard thumping and scratching sounds.

Locked windows and doors opened and closed on their own.

Swarms of houseflies mysteriously appeared.

A devil-like creature was seen outside the window at night.

The temperature in the house would go from hot to freezing cold.

The toilet water turned black.

Green slime oozed out of the walls and ceiling.

Household objects moved about on their own.

317

HOW TO READ TEA LEAVES

Learn the ancient Chinese art of tasseography
and unlock the secrets of your future.

SUPPLIES

• A plain, light colored tea cup and saucer. Make sure the cup has a wide opening and narrow base.

• A teaspoon of loose tea

• Hot water

INSTRUCTIONS

1. Put the loose tea in an empty cup. (If you have only tea bags, cut open two bags and pour the contents into the cup.)

2. Fill cup with hot water. Let the tea steep for a few minutes.

3. Sip the tea. While you're drinking, think of a question.

4. Stop drinking before you get to the last few drops of tea. There should be one or two teaspoons of liquid and the tea leaves at the bottom of cup.

5. Swirl the cup counterclockwise three times with your left hand (or right hand if you're left-handed).

6. Immediately after swirling, turn the cup over onto the saucer. Drain the liquid. Then turn the cup over with the handle pointing toward you.

READING THE TEA LEAVES:

1. The handle is Home. Anything you see here is bound to strike close to home.

2. The rim is the Present.

3. The walls are the Immediate Future.

4. The bottom is the Distant Future.

Reading tea leaves is like seeing shapes in the clouds. Use the guide below to interpret the shapes. Start at the handle and work your way down to the bottom.

TASSEOGRAPHY "SYMBOLS"

Elephant: Wisdom

Bird: Good news

Mountain: An obstacle or challenge

Sun: Joy and power

Moon: Fame and riches

Airplane or train: Travel

Eyeglasses: Study the situation thoroughly

Octopus: Overwhelming; too much to do

Fish: Good news from far away

Heart: Love

Cat: Treachery

Key: Problem solved

Knot: An argument

Lock: Something to be solved or opened

Volcano: A situation about to erupt

Coins: Prosperity

Mouse: Thief nearby

Letters: First letter of someone's name

Spider: Unexpected inheritance

Dog: Faithful friend

Clouds: Wishes coming true

Teardrop: Disappointment or sadness

WILL POWER

People have left some pretty strange requests in their wills.

HAPPY BIRTHDAY TO YOU

Robert Louis Stevenson, the author of *Treasure Island*, left his birthday to a good friend who had always complained about being born on Christmas.

A CLASS ACT

Edwin Forrest was a leading stage actor in the 1800s who left all his money to the Actors Fund to establish a retirement home for his fellow actors. But he had two conditions: 1) They had to do a reading of Shakespeare on Shakespeare's birthday; and 2) The Declaration of Independence had to be read every 4th of July.

TAKE THAT!

An Australian named Lord Francis Reginal left one shilling to his wife "for tram fare so she can go somewhere and drown herself."

NO MONKEYING AROUND

Patricia O'Neill got angry at her husband and left her estate to her chimp, Kalu. The ape's take: $100 million!

MONEY FOR HER MAKER

A woman in Cherokee County, North Carolina, left her entire estate to God. The court told the county sheriff to try to find the beneficiary. A few days later the sheriff returned and submitted this report: "After due and diligent search, God cannot be found in this county."

HIGHWAY TO HEAVEN

Sandra West was a wealthy socialite from Beverly Hills who left her brother $3 million, provided that he buried her in her lace nightgown and sitting in her Ferrari, with the seat at a comfortable slant. So that's what he did—but then he poured concrete over the Ferrari so no one would be tempted to dig her up and drive the car away.

BIG AND SMALL

The world's longest will was 95,000 words long. The tiniest will was written on the back of a postage stamp.

PUSHING UP DAISIES

These are from real gravestones—really!

Here lies
Ann Mann,

Who lived
an old maid

But died an
old Mann.

Here lies
the body of
Jonathan Blake

Stepped
on the gas

Instead of the brake.

Here lies
Lester Moore

Four slugs
from a .44

No Les
No More.

Stranger,

Tread this ground
with gravity;

Dentist Brown
is filling

His last cavity!

THE HAUNTED PAINTING

On February 2, 2000, a California couple put a very strange item up for sale on eBay: a haunted painting. An art dealer originally found the painting behind an abandoned brewery and sold it to them. They hung the 24- by 36-inch painting in their living room...and that's when the trou-ble began. One morn-ing their four-year-old daughter announced that the "children in the picture were fight-ing." The couple claimed to have caught the ghosts in the painting in action with a motion-trig-gered camera. And now they wanted to get rid of it.

As word of the auc-tion spread across the Web, more than 13,000 people viewed

the painting. Some people swore that looking at it made them physically ill, as if they were possessed by an evil spirit. No one knows what the family originally paid for the picture, but they sold it for $1,025.

GOT GHOSTS?

Think there may be ghosts in your house?
Here's how experts say you can tell.

TEN TELLTALE SIGNS THAT YOUR HOUSE IS HAUNTED

• You feel a cool breeze even though the windows are closed.

• You hear voices that come from nowhere and you feel like someone is watching you.

• You hear footsteps walking in and out of empty rooms.

• You smell roses, oranges, or an "electric" odor.

• Jewelry, shoes, tools, and other small items are moved from one location to another…but nobody (nobody human, that is) moved them.

• Lights and electrical appliances turn on and off by themselves.

• Your bedcovers are thrown off you.

• You feel a warm touch on your back or shoulders. (The touch of a ghost is always warm, never cold.)

• You receive repeat phone calls from a caller who never identifies himself.

• You see flashes of light or movement out of the corner of your eye, yet when you look there's nothing there.

GHOSTBUSTING TIPS

Okay, so you know you've got ghosts. Now what do you do? Here are five tips.

1. TALK TO THE GHOST. Let him know that this is your house and he must stop bothering you or leave immediately. Shout if you must.

2. SHOE SHUFFLE. Put your shoes at the foot of your bed, with one shoe pointing one way and the other pointing in the opposite direction. This confuses the ghosts and they leave.

3. GET THE DIRT. Take a scoop of dirt from the path to your front door and dump it in a nearby graveyard. The ghosts will follow.

4. PAINT YOUR FRONT DOOR RED. Ghosts won't enter a home with a red door.

5. GET OUT THE VACUUM. If all else fails, clean your house. Ghosts don't like clean homes.

SOLD!

Surfing the Internet? Some pretty strange things are being sold on eBay.

ITEM: A ghost and his former cane.

STORY: Mary Anderson placed her father's "ghost" up for auction when her son, Collin, told her that his grandpa had come back to haunt him. She had only one request for the winning bidder: "I would like you to write a letter after you've received the cane (and the ghost) to my son, letting him know that his grandfather is there with you and you're getting along great."

SOLD: $65,000

ITEM: Grilled cheese sandwich.

STORY: This sandwich was saved in a refrigerator for ten years because it

appeared to bear the image of the Virgin Mary.
SOLD: $28,000

ITEM: Leftover french toast
STORY: It's Justin Timberlake's partially eaten french toast (with extra syrup) plus the fork and plate he used when he was appearing on the Z100 morning radio show.
SOLD: $3,154

ITEM: "Stuff Found in Couch"
STORY: Found while looking for TV remote: three pieces of Big Red chewing gum, a screw, 80¢, two rubber bands, a peppermint candy, a paper clip, a red cap from a Bic pen, a wrapper from a Starburst candy, a partial box of matches, the edge of a piece of paper from a spiral bound notebook, a few shards from a pecan shell, and a third of a pretzel.
SOLD: $3.06 (plus $3.20 shipping)

ITEM: A piece of Nutri-Grain cereal with the image of E.T.
STORY: The E.T. grain was rescued from a bowl of cereal seconds before the milk was poured on it.
SOLD: $1,035

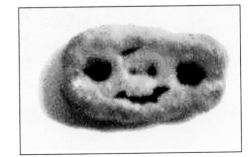

A-TISKET, A-TASKET

Some strange and scary caskets!

CAN YOU HEAR ME NOW? Want to talk to a deceased loved one but feel silly muttering at a mound of dirt? Now you can call directly into their casket with the new Telephonic Angel. The system has a loudspeaker that was designed by Juergen Broether as a way to talk to his mother who died in 1998.

PROFESSIONAL BOXERS. In Ghana, clients of Isaac Sowah and other fantasy coffin makers like to go out in style. Some choose a coffin that reflects their line of business: a shoemaker may want to be buried in a large shoe or a fisherman in a big fish. Others choose elephants, eagles, airplanes, or even mobile phones. Sowah says cars are very popular, especially Mercedes and Cadillacs.

DUMB CROOKS

These guys are one taco short of a "combo plate."

IT'S IN THE BAG...OR NOT

In Portland, Oregon, a man attempted to rob a bank by slipping a note to the teller. The note read: "This is a holdup, and I've got a gun. Put all the money in a paper bag." The teller refused to give him the money and wrote this note back to the man: "I don't have a paper bag."

GET A GRIP

If you're going to steal groceries there's one thing you should remember: don't stuff a lobster in your underwear. That's what Winston Treadway did, and was he sorry! He had already crammed a number of food items in his clothes and was sneaking toward the exit when a giant claw clamped down on his private parts. His cries of pain attracted the grocery clerks, who immediately called the police. The police arrested Winston, who was still in the lobster's grip. They finally had to use a set of pliers to pry open the angry lobster's claw.

RING-A-DING-DING

When a guy in Michigan tried to rob a Burger King, the clerk at the counter told him he couldn't open the cash register without a food order. So the would-be robber ordered onion rings. When the clerk told him that it was still breakfast time and onion rings were not yet available, the guy gave up and went home.

PICK ME!

When Los Angeles detectives asked each man in a police lineup to repeat the words, "Give me all your money or I'll shoot," the real robber shouted, "That's not what I said!" He was promptly thrown in jail.

FILL 'ER UP

When two gas station attendants in Iona, Michigan, refused to give a drunken robber any money, the drunk threatened to call the cops. They still refused, so the tipsy thief called the police, who came...and arrested him.

SIGN IN PLEASE

In 1987 five teenagers were arrested for spray painting graffiti all over the Lincoln Memorial in Washington, D.C. How did the police know who did it? The culprits spray painted their names on the monument.

ALPHABET SOUP

Ready for some wordplay? Letter rip!

• If the English alphabet was lined up in the order of most commonly used letters to the least used, it would look like this: E T A I S O N H R D L U C M F W Y P G V B K J Q X Z

• The first word spoken on the moon was "Okay."

• No words rhyme with *orange*, *purple*, or *month*.

• *Taphephobia* is the fear of being buried alive.

• Q is the only letter in the alphabet that doesn't appear in any of the names of the 50 United States.

• The most common name in the world: Muhammad.

• Smokey the Bear's original name was "Hot Foot Teddy."

• *Set* has more definitions than any other word.

• Compulsive nose picking is called *rhinotillexomania*.

• *Pants* was considered a dirty word in England in the 1880s.

• The world's longest place name is in New Zealand. *Taumatawhakatangihangakoauauotamateaturipukakapikimaungahoronukupokaiwhenuakitanatahu* is Maori and means, "The brow of the hill where Tamatea—the man with the big knees who slid down, climbed up, and swallowed mountains, traveled the land and is known as the Land Eater—played his nose flute to his loved one."

WEIRD WORLD OF SPORTS

Beyond baseball, basketball, and football.

EXTREME CROQUET

It's more than just using mallets to hit balls through wickets—extreme croquet involves trees, cliffs, water hazards, mud, vines, and great distances. Started in the 1920s, a group of Swedish students perfected it in 1975. Now it has mallets that look more like sledgehammers, two-story-tall wickets, and balls that are able to withstand a good strong *thwack* in the deep, dark woods. (Cheating is encouraged.)

SHIN KICKING

Also known as "purring" in Wales, here's how it's played: Two men stand face to face with their hands on each other's shoulders. They wear reinforced shoes. At the signal, they start kicking each other's shins until one loses his grip on his opponent. (This sport has failed to catch on in other nations.)

TOE WRESTLING

The World Championships are held each year in a pub in Wetton, England. The contestants sit on the floor with their right foot down and left foot in the air. They lock toes and attempt to press their opponent's foot to the floor. (If a player is in too much pain, he is allowed to stop the proceedings by yelling "Toe much!")

WIFE CARRYING

It's the extreme sport of choice in Finland.
A man carries his wife over a 780-foot course,
through water, sand, and grass and
over fences. Dropping your wife
results in a 15-second
penalty. The prize?
The wife's weight
in lemonade.

AMAZING COINCIDENCES

Strange things are happening!

LUCK OF THE IRISH. For years, Mrs. Coyle of Glasgow, Scotland, carried a lucky sixpence with her initials on it. The day before she went to Ireland she accidentally spent it. She was heartbroken…until two days later when, while shopping in a small Irish village, the coin with her initials was given back to her in change.

LOTS OF STOTTS. In 1985 John Stott crashed his car. The accident was witnessed by Bernard Stott. The investigator on the scene was Tina Stott. All three Stotts went to the police station where they met desk sergeant Walter Stott. None of the Stotts were related.

BETTER LATE THAN DEAD. On March 1, 1950, a church choir in Beatrice, Nebraska, cheated death by an amazing stroke of luck. The 15 singers met at the same time every week for practice—7:15 p.m.—but that night everyone was late. One had car trouble, another wanted to hear the end of a radio show, another had to finish some chores at home. That's why no one was inside the church when a gas leak caused an explosion at 7:25.

HAIL TO THE CHIEFS. Three of the first five presidents of the United States—John Adams, Thomas Jefferson, and James Monroe—all died on the same day of the year: July 4th.

THE TRAVELING PANTS

The gift that kept on giving.

Larry Kunkel didn't like the pants his mother gave him for Christmas in 1964. So the next Christmas, Kunkel wrapped them and gave them to his brother-in-law, Roy Collette. But Collette didn't want them either. So he gave the pants back to Kunkel the following year. The men continued this friendly back and forth gift exchange for the next 10 years...and then the rules changed.

In 1974 Collette stuffed the pants into a three-foot-long, one-inch pipe, and gave the pipe to Kunkel, who accepted the challenge. The two men traded the pants back and forth for another 15 years, each time finding more clever ways to deliver them. They were delivered in a four-ton concrete Rubik's Cube, locked inside a 600-pound safe, cemented into a monster tire, and put in the backseat of a car that was then crushed into a three-foot cube.

There was only one rule to Collette and Kunkel's gift exchange: if the pants were damaged, the game would stop. In 1989 the pants caught fire and burned when Collette tried to encase them in 10,000 pounds of glass. That year Kunkel received a brass urn filled with ashes and a note.

> Sorry, Old Man, here lies the pants...
> An attempt to cast the pants in glass
> Brought about their demise at last.

The urn now graces Larry Kunkel's fireplace mantel.

DUMB JOCKS

"Did I say that?"

"The doctors X-rayed my head and found nothing."

—Dizzy Dean, Hall of Fame pitcher, after getting beaned

"Sure I've got one. It's a perfect 20–20."
—Duane Thomas, Dallas Cowboys running back, on his IQ

"My grandmother told me it was good for colds."
—Kevin Mitchell, outfielder, on why he eats Vicks VapoRub

"He's a guy who gets up at six o'clock in the morning regardless of what time it is."
—Lou Duva, boxing trainer, on heavyweight Andrew Golota

"Are you any relation to your brother Marv?"
—Leon Wood, basketball player, to announcer Steve Albert

"Better make it six—I can't eat eight."
—Dan Osinski, pitcher, when asked if he wanted his pizza cut into six or eight slices

"Left hand, right hand, it doesn't matter. I'm amphibious."
—Charles Shackleford, North Carolina State basketball player

POTTY MOUTH

The city of Amsterdam in the Netherlands has toilets that actually talk.

Artist Leonard van Munster has created a toilet that gives advice, warns of germs, and makes fun of you for not washing your hands. It's been installed in the Café de Balie bathroom… and anyone who makes a pit stop there will get an earful. The toilet, which is wired with sensors connected to a computer, senses what's happening in the room and responds accordingly. One reporter heard a female voice tell him, "You might consider sitting down next time." The next person was given this warning: "The last visitor did not take heed of basic rules of hygiene." Those who think they can sneak off to the bathroom for a cigarette get a big surprise when the toilet suddenly starts coughing and warns them of the hazards of smoking.

EXTREME IRONING

A strange new sport is born.

One sunny afternoon in 1997 Englishman Phil Shaw looked at his pile of wrinkled clothes and wondered how could he stay inside ironing on such a beautiful day. That's when he decided to combine his least favorite chore with his favorite pastime, rock climbing.

Not long after his first ironing adventure, Phil, known in extreme ironing circles as "Steam," convinced his roommate, "Spray," to join him. While the two ironers practiced their sport, they refined the rules of competition and recruited new athletes for ironing while rock climbing, sailing, and even scuba diving. And it took off: In 2002, 80 different teams from 10 different countries competed in the Extreme Ironing World Championship.

UGLY IS BEAUTIFUL

Gurning: the art of making ugly faces.

E very year since 1267, the town of Egremont, England, has hosted the World Gurning Championship. Men, women, and children cross their eyes, blow out their cheeks, suck in their noses, or twist their mouths to make the grossest face possible. Ugly is beautiful at the World Gurning Championship. But gurning's not about coming into the contest ugly. Being naturally ugly won't make a competitor an automatic winner. Champion gurners know how to transform their faces into grotesque masks without the help of their hands or artificial aids. (Hint: It helps to be toothless.)

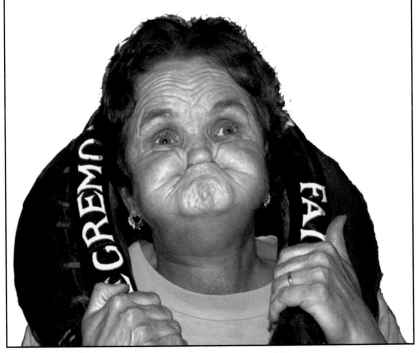

PACKRATS

Who are the most infamous hoarders in history?

NORMAL BEGINNINGS

Homer and Langley Collyer were born into a wealthy New York family in the 1880s. Their father was a well-known doctor and their mother an opera singer. Both boys were raised to be gentlemen and scholars. Homer became an engineer and musician, while Langley was a lawyer. They lived and prospered together in a luxurious three-story mansion in Harlem. And then something snapped.

By 1910 Harlem was becoming a rough, crime-ridden neighborhood. And the worse it got, the more the Collyer brothers retreated into their home. They boarded up the windows, booby-trapped the doors, and shut off their utilities. Then they stopped going out in the daytime and started wandering the neighborhood after midnight. They dug through trash cans for food, gathered water from a pipe four blocks from their home, and began collecting strange stuff—car parts, sewing machines, mannequins, rusted bicycles, broken baby carriages, and junk for their boobytraps. (Langley built a system of booby traps that would dump mountains of trash on top of any intruder.)

HERMIT HIDEOUT

For 33 years, the hermits of Harlem lived behind closed doors, never letting anyone into their lives. Even when Homer became blind and paralyzed from a stroke, they stayed hidden inside their fortress. Langley, convinced Homer's sight would return if he just ate enough oranges, began stockpiling newspapers—thousands and thousands of them—for Homer to read when he regained his sight.

OPEN SESAME

On March 21, 1947, the police received a call that there was a dead man in the Collyer home. It took them more than 24 hours to dig through the trash to get in—every door and window they pried open was fortified by mountains of magazines, broken furniture, suitcases, chandeliers, and trash. They finally found Homer, dead in his chair (he had died of starvation). But where was Langley?

The search began. Every room in the house was crammed floor to ceiling with an outrageous collection of rubbish that included an X-ray machine, dressmakers' dummies, medical specimens in jars, a horse buggy, two pipe organs, a cache of weapons, and 14 grand pianos. Tunnels and crawlspaces were carved into the mountains of junk. Finally, after 18 days of searching, the police found Langley, only a few feet from his brother, buried under a ton of trash—a victim of one of his booby traps. He had died trying to deliver his brother's dinner.

THE STUFF

In the end, 136 tons of trash were hauled away. The Collyer mansion was torn down and turned into a parking lot, but the Collyer legend lives on. Even today, New York City firefighters who get an emergency call to a junk-jammed apartment say, "We got another Collyer."

FASHION POLICE

You can't wear that! It's too weird!

CRIME: In 1750 Jonas Hanway was one of the first men to carry an umbrella in London. Before that time only women carried them.

PUNISHMENT: People on the streets jeered at him.

CRIME: John Hetherington wore the world's very first top hat (also on the streets of London) in the 1800s.

PUNISHMENT: He was arrested for "frightening the public" and fined £50 (today's equivalent: $2,500).

CRIME: In 1907 Australian swimming star Annette Kellerman wore a one-piece bathing suit that revealed her knees and exposed her elbows.

PUNISHMENT: She was arrested for indecent exposure.

THE ELEPHANT MAN

He's been called the saddest man who ever lived. A hundred years after his death, his memory lives on.

Joseph Merrick was born in Leicester, England, in August 1862. At two, the tumors that would disfigure him began to grow. A hunk of flesh that hung from his forehead resembled an elephant's trunk, which gave him his nickname—the Elephant Man. He had a deformed nose and a hand that looked like a fin, and his body was hung with sacs of wrinkled skin. People called him a monster, but Merrick was an intelligent, gentle person who loved to read and write poetry.

When a popular surgeon named Frederick Treves gave him a home at Whitechapel Hospital in London, Merrick became famous. The toast of London society came to visit him, marveling at the beautiful soul that lived beneath the hideous face. The Elephant Man, whose spine was so twisted he could barely walk, died in his sleep in 1890. He was 27 years old.

SCARY JOKES

These jokes are monstrous!

Q: What do you call a haunted chicken?
A: A poultry-geist

Q: What's a ghost's favorite road?
A: A dead end

Q: Why do vampires brush their teeth?
A: To get rid of bat breath

Q: What do you call a ghost's mom and dad?
A: Transparents

Q: Who should you call when a pumpkin dies?
A: The next of pump–kin

Q: Where do ghosts play tennis?
A: On a tennis corpse

Q: What would you call the ghost of a door-to-door salesman?
A: A dead ringer

Q: How do vampires travel?
A: By blood vessel

Q: What do you get when you cross a were-wolf with a snowball?
A: Frostbite

TONGUE-TIED PROFESSOR

This is what happens when your brain runs faster than your tongue.

Reverend William Archibald Spooner (1844–1930) was Dean of New College in Oxford, England. He was a short albino with a head too big for his body. But it wasn't his looks that set him apart from others—it was the way he mixed up his words.

He once fumbled a toast to Queen Victoria when he raised his glass and said, "We must drink a toast to our queer old dean." And during a wedding, Spooner told the groom, "Son, it is now kisstomary to cuss the bride."

Reverend Spooner made so many memorable tongue-twisting mistakes that the tendency was named after him.

SPOONERISMS

He Meant To Say...	But He Said...
You have wasted two terms.	"You have tasted two worms."
Which of us in his heart has not felt a half-formed wish?	"Which of us in his heart has not felt a half-warmed fish?"
Is the dean busy?	"Is the bean dizzy?"
Pardon me Madam, this pew is occupied. May I show you to another seat?	"Mardon me padam, this pie is occupewed. May I sew you to another sheet?"

GERM WARFARE

Watch out! They're everywhere!

IN THE BATHROOM...

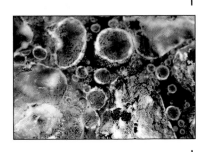

• Every time you flush, water mists into the air and 600,000 bacteria land on everything within six feet of the bowl, including your toothbrush, makeup, hairbrush, and towel.

• Also living in your towels: bacteria and fungus from dead skin.

• One bacteria cell in your loofah can sprout into a billion overnight.

IN THE LIVING ROOM...

• Your couch is crawling with dust mites.

• The household dust on your shelves and coffee table is mostly dead skin.

• Old newspapers are covered in bacteria.

• Watch out for doorknobs and telephones! Danger! Danger! Viruses!

IN THE KITCHEN...

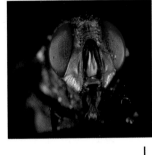

• Your sink is germ heaven. Especially for deadly bacteria like *salmonella* and *campylobacter*.

• Use dishtowels once and bacteria begin growing immediately.

• *Yersinia* bacteria, which causes diarrhea, can be found inside your refrigerator.

• Bacteria from raw meat and unwashed produce live on your cutting board.

IN THE BEDROOM...

• As many as two million dust mites can call one double bed home.

• Dust mites and spiders love the inside of a closet.

• Watch out for your computer keyboard and mouse! Danger! Danger! Viruses!

ON YOUR PETS...

• Dogs can carry salmonella, ticks, fleas, poison oak, and poison ivy.

• Cats can carry parasites like ring worm, roundworm, and *toxoplasma*.

LUCKY FINDS #2

Some people have all the luck...like these guys.

FOUND: A winning ticket

WHERE: In a cactus tree

THE STORY: Evans Kamande, a 17-year-old Kenyan, was playing in a park in Nairobi when suddenly he had to "go." So he found a spot—a nearby cactus tree—and noticed a little box stuck in the fork of the plant's branches. Inside the box: the winning ticket in a treasure hunt sponsored by a local radio station...worth $5,000!

FOUND: A legendary baseball

WHERE: Grandma's attic

THE STORY: In 1996 a New Jersey kid named Mark Scala told his 87-year-old grandmother that he wanted to be Babe Ruth for a school project. She remembered that her late husband had won a signed Babe Ruth baseball back in 1927 when he made the all-state baseball team. Sure enough, they found the ball in an old box up in her attic and were stunned to find out it was the ball from Babe Ruth's very first home run in Yankee Stadium. They sold it in 1998 for $126,500.

THE FIND: A precious gem

WHERE: A mine in North Carolina

THE STORY: Ten-year-old Larry Shields was poking through a bucket of dirt that had been thrown away by a commercial gem mine near his home. He found an interesting rock and decided to keep it because he "liked the shape." Good idea—it turned out to be a 1,061-carat sapphire worth more than $35,000.

THE FIND: A Wendy's cup worth $200,000

WHERE: In the garbage

THE STORY: A sharp-eyed trash collector named Craig Randall from Peabody, Massachusetts, was loading some garbage into his truck when he spotted a Wendy's contest cup sticking out of a trash bag. "I won a chicken sandwich the week before," he said later, "and I figured, hey, I'd get some fries to go with it." When he peeled off the sticker he found a message that read, "Congratulations. You have won $200,000 towards a new home."

THE FIND: The Declaration of Independence

WHERE: Inside a picture frame

THE STORY: In 1989 a Philadelphia man paid $4 for a painting at a flea market, just because he liked the frame. As he was removing the picture from the frame, a piece of folded-up paper fell out. It was a copy of the Declaration of Independence, yellowed with age but otherwise in good condition. The man took it to Sotheby's auction house, where it was found to be one of the original copies from 1776. It sold for a cool $8.14 million.

BABYSITTER TOPS THE CHARTS

Davy Crockett's niece was only a teenager when she wrote America's best-known lullaby.

In 1872 a 15-year-old girl named Effie Crockett was babysitting a very fussy baby. Trying to calm him down, Effie sang a tune, using the words to an old nursery rhyme. The song worked like a charm. Later, when Effie was given a banjo for Christmas, she plucked out the melody for her music teacher. He liked it so much he sent her to a music publisher in Boston, who liked it, too. Effie

wrote some more verses, the lullaby was published— and it was a hit. Now, more than a hundred years later, babysitters still croon Effie's tune to restless children:

*Rock-a-bye baby
on the treetop,
When the wind blows,
the cradle will rock.
When the
bough breaks,
the cradle will fall,
And down will come
baby, cradle and all.*

STRANGE AND SILLY RECORDS

What will they think of next?

LEAPFROGGING: In 1991 fourteen students from Stanford University leapfrogged their way to a new world distance record when they hopped 996 miles—almost the entire length of California. (It took them more than 13 days to do it.)

VW BUG CRAMMING: The record was broken on April 29, 2000, when 25 people in Kremser, Austria, stuffed themselves into a new Volkswagen Beetle.

PILLOW FIGHTING: On September 29, 2004, 2,773 warriors (and their pillows) met in Dodgeville, Wisconsin, for the largest pillow fight in history.

WHOOPEE CUSHIONSITTING: In March 2004, 3,614 people simultaneously sat down on whoopee cushions for the biggest-ever whoopee fart-a-thon.

GROUCHO-ING: On June 2005, the Toukey Junior Rugby Club set a new world record for the largest "Groucho Gathering" when 1,437 members of the team crowded onto Darren Kennedy Field in NSW, Australia wearing Groucho Marx–style glasses, noses, and moustaches.

DID YOU KNOW?

A few odd facts to entertain your friends and family.

• After the Pilgrim ship *Mayflower* sailed to America, it was taken apart and made into a barn.

• Benjamin Franklin invented the rocking chair.

• A whistle sounds louder just before it rains.

• The electric chair was invented by a dentist.

• Shelby Park, born on February 10, 2001, was the first baby to have her birth broadcast live on the Internet.

• Most lipstick contains fish scales.

• In 1996 the Boy Scouts created the new "Public Relations Skills" merit badge. (It has a cell phone on it.)

• Some women in Costa Rica decorate their hair with chains of glowing fireflies.

• In Leonardo da Vinci's famous portrait, Mona Lisa has no eyebrows.

• While it was being developed, the Segway scooter had a top secret code name: Ginger.

• President Andrew Jackson believed the earth was flat.

• Alexander Graham Bell, inventor of the telephone, never called his wife or mother…because they were both deaf.

ROYAL PIG OUT

If you could eat anything you wanted...

VITELLIUS (AD 15–69). This Roman emperor once served 2,000 fish and 7,000 birds at one single feast. His strangest, most famous dish—called "The Shield of Minerva"—consisted of fish livers mixed with peacock brains, tossed with flamingo tongues and the guts of lamprey eels.

HELIOGABALUS (AD 203–222). Only 14 when he became emperor of Rome, he loved to throw huge feasts. Favorite dishes were made of camel's heels, small rodents, and powdered glass. He once served 600 roasted ostriches (with brains), and then dropped so many roses from a false ceiling that some guests drowned in the blossoms.

NEBUCHADNEZZAR II (605–562 BC). He built the Hanging Gardens of Babylon—one of the Seven Wonders of the Ancient World. But this king had much simpler tastes than the Romans. He ate grass. Why? According to legend, he thought he was a goat.

BODY PARTS

Some famous people didn't go to their graves with all of their parts. Here's why.

MISSING BODY PART: Albert Einstein's brain
FOUND: Under a kitchen sink in Kansas.
HOW IT GOT THERE: Einstein had asked that his friend Dr. Harry Zimmerman examine his brain after he died. So during the autopsy following Einstein's death in 1955, pathologist Dr. Thomas Harvey removed Einstein's brain, cut it into 200 pieces, and gave some of it to Zim-

merman as Einstein had requested. But Harvey took the rest to his home in Lawrence, Kansas. For the next 40 years, Harvey stored Einstein's brain in jars filled with formaldehyde under his kitchen sink, occasionally giving out specimens to research scientists. One scientist kept his portion of Einstein's brain in his refrigerator in a jar marked "Big Al's Brain."

MISSING BODY PART: Galileo's middle finger

FOUND: In an Italian museum

HOW IT GOT THERE: Galileo
Galilei was an Italian scientist who
made important discoveries in physics
and astronomy. In 1737, nearly a century after his death, Galileo's body
was being moved from a storage closet
to a mausoleum, and a nobleman
named Anton Francesco Gori cut off three fingers as a
souvenir. The middle finger was eventually acquired by
the Museum of the History of Science in Florence, Italy.
(The other two fingers are in a private collection.)

MISSING BODY PART: Buddha's teeth

FOUND: In Beijing, China, and Taipei, Taiwan

HOW THEY GOT THERE: Legend has it that two
teeth found in Buddha's cremated remains after his death
2,400 years ago were taken to temples in the Far East.

MISSING BODY PART: Stonewall Jackson's arm

FOUND: On an old battlefield in Virginia

HOW IT GOT THERE: In 1863, at the height of the
Civil War, Confederate general Jackson was accidentally
shot by his own troops. A bullet hit his left arm, which
then had to be amputated above the elbow. His troops
buried the arm in a nearby field, complete with a reli-
gious ceremony and a marble tombstone. When Jackson
died from complications eight days later, the rest of him
was buried in Lexington, Virginia.

GHOSTLY HITCHHIKERS

Here are three good reasons
not to pick up hitchhikers.

THE GHOST OF HIGHWAY 48

In South Carolina, worried motorists reported seeing a young girl carrying a suitcase walking along Highway 48. When the drivers offered her a ride, she told them she was going to visit her sick mother in Columbia. She gave them the address and as they got to the outskirts of Columbia, she suddenly disappeared. One couple who picked her up went to the address and described the girl to a man who lived there. He replied that it was his sister and that she had been killed by a hit-and-run driver in the 1950s while walking to visit their sick mother.

NOW YOU SEE HER—NOW YOU DON'T

Frightened bus drivers in Taiwan have refused to drive to a remote village outside of T'ai-nan because of one ghostly girl. Drivers report stopping at a shadowy area near a sugarcane plantation. A young girl gets on the bus but never gets off. She simply vanishes before the bus gets to town.

RESURRECTION MARY

Nearly every year on the anniversary of her death, a blond-haired, blue-eyed girl in a flowing dress can be seen standing on the side of Archer Road in Chicago. Some unsuspecting drivers think she's hitchhiking or in trouble and offer to give her a ride. They report that she gets into the car and says, "I have to go home." When the car nears the gates to Resurrection Cemetery, she cries, "Here! Stop here!" and simply disappears into thin air. It seems that Mary had been to a dance at the O'Henry Ballroom in the 1930s. When she got in a fight with her boyfriend, she left the dance and started to walk home. On a curve along Archer Road, near Resurrection Cemetery, Mary was killed by a hit-and-run driver. For 75 years, Mary's ghost has been doomed to wander the dark stretch of road looking for "a ride home."

THE WHO?

Where do rock bands get those strange names?

LIMP BIZKIT. Singer Fred Durst got the idea from his dog, Biscuit, who has a limp.

SMASH MOUTH. Taken from the slang term football players use for any game with a lot of blocking or tackling.

THIRD EYE BLIND. It's said that our "third eye" is the imagined one that gives us a sixth sense. The band felt that when it comes to ESP, most humans are blind.

HOOBASTANK was a word the band members invented when they were in high school. They used it as slang to describe everything.

NICKELBACK got their name from bass player Mike Kroeger, who once worked at Starbucks in Vancouver. At the time, most coffee drinks cost $2.95, $3.95, or $4.95. Kroeger got so used to saying, "Here's your nickel back," that when the band was trying to come up with a name, all he could think of was the phrase "nickel back."

THE WHO. The group, first called The High Numbers, was looking for a new name. Every time someone came up with an idea, they jokingly asked, "The *who?*" Finally a friend said, "Why not just call yourselves 'The Who'?" So they did.

LIZARD MAN

Erik Sprague loves lizards. In fact, he loves them so much that he has spent almost 650 hours (spread over 10 years) in tattoo parlors, transforming himself into a "lizard man." Some of the changes: Sprague was one of the first people to have his tongue surgically forked like a lizard's. Then he had little Teflon balls implanted in his brow. He went on to have his face, eyelids, and most of his body tattooed and pierced to make him look even more lizardlike.

Sprague, who was a National Merit Scholar finalist, now tours in his own "freak" show, where he eats fire, swallows swords, gobbles live worms, and shoots darts out of his nose. His plans for the future? A tail implant.

359

RIDICULOUS RECORDS

LONGEST DISTANCE RUN BACKWARD

In 1984 Arvind Pandya of India ran backward 3,178 miles, from Los Angeles to New York, in 107 days.

FARTHEST SPAGHETTI NOSE BLOW

On December 16, 1998, with a single blow, Kevin Cole of Carlsbad, New Mexico, blew a strand of spaghetti out of his nose for a record distance of 7.5 inches.

BIGGEST BUBBLE GUM BUBBLE

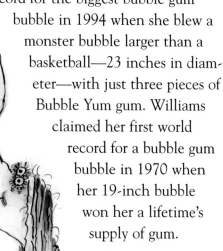

Susan Montgomery Williams claimed her fourth world record for the biggest bubble gum bubble in 1994 when she blew a monster bubble larger than a basketball—23 inches in diameter—with just three pieces of Bubble Yum gum. Williams claimed her first world record for a bubble gum bubble in 1970 when her 19-inch bubble won her a lifetime's supply of gum.

FASTEST RUMPJUMP

David Fisher of Chicago, Illinois, set a world record in 1998, when he "rumpjumped" 56 times in one minute. What's a rumpjump? Jumping over a jumprope with only your butt.

TALLEST GOLF BALL TOWER

On October 4, 1998, Don Athey of Bridgeport, Ohio, broke the record for building a golf ball tower when he stacked nine balls on top of each other without using any kind of glue.

GREATEST TONGUE-TIE

On January 26, 1999, Al Gliniecki of Gulf Breeze, Florida, tied 39 cherry stems into knots in a record three minutes…using his tongue.

LONGEST DOMINO SETUP

China's Ma Li Hua single-handedly set up the greatest number of dominoes ever—303,628 tiles snaked through a massive maze that covered the floor of the Singapore Expo Hall in Singapore. And then, on August 18, 2003, she toppled them. (All but seven of the dominoes fell over.)

MOST GLASSES BALANCED ON CHIN

On April 26, 2001, Ashrita Furman of New York City balanced 75 pint beer glasses on his chin for 10.6 seconds.

BLACK HOLES

We can't see them. We can't feel them.
But we know they're there.

WHAT ARE THEY?

The bigger a star, the stronger its force of gravity. When a big star explodes (astronomers call that a *supernova*), its dust is scattered throughout the universe. All that's left is a gigantic gravitational force called a *black hole*.

A black hole is like a cosmic vacuum cleaner that sucks everything into it, even other stars. How do we know black holes are out there? Astronomers can see the swirling gases of other stars being sucked toward the blackness. It looks like water going down a drain.

The swirling gases around a black hole go so fast that they get superheated. This causes them to give off X-rays. That was the clue that led to the discovery of the first black hole. In 1970 astronomers detected X-rays coming from an area near a distant star. They expected to find another, even bigger star. But the area emitting the X-rays didn't shine—it was pitch black and 10 times bigger than our sun. Astronomers named the mysterious black spot Cygnus X-1.

BLACK HOLE FACTS

• Black holes can grow. The more stars they swallow, the bigger they get.

• Black holes can swallow *other* black holes.

• There is a black hole right at the heart of our own galaxy, the Milky Way. *Gulp!*

TRY IT...
YOU'LL LIKE IT!

RAT-A-TOOEY

Quang Li-Do has been catching and eating rats for 30 years. He likes them so much that he opened a restaurant in Canton, China, that specializes in rat cuisine. Every year the Jailu Restaurant serves more than 7,500 rats to its satisfied customers!

SALSA STINGER

Some people can't live without chocolate. Others love cheese. But Rene Alvarenga of Intipucá, El Salvador, has a very different craving—scorpions. Live ones! Every day, he snarfs down 20 to 30 of them. He claims to have eaten more than 35,000 in his lifetime.

ROACH BEEF

Entertainer Ken Edwards will do anything for attention. He once stuffed 47 live rats into a pair of pantyhose—while he was wearing them. Then, on March 5, 2001, on live TV, he attempted to break a world record by eating 36 cockroaches in one minute. (He did it!)

MAKE A OUIJA

Want to know what the future holds? Ask the Ouija.

WHAT IS IT? Communicating with "spirits" was a big fad in 19th-century America. Starting in the 1890s you could buy talking boards—called Ouija boards—to speak to them. One manufacturer, Charles Kennard, claimed the board itself told him the word *ouija* was Egyptian for good luck. Another, William Fuld, said the name was a blend of the French and German words for "yes"—*oui* and *ja*. Whatever it means, millions of people have given themselves creepy thrills playing with Ouija boards. Do they really work? You decide.

WHAT YOU NEED TO MAKE ONE:

- A sheet of white cardboard or art board
- Colored pens or pencils
- A small jar or glass
- Lots of imagination

BEFORE YOU BEGIN:

1. Be sure to leave lots of room around the edges of your board so that the pointer doesn't fall off when it moves to a symbol.

2. It is very important that your board is flat and smooth so the pointer can slide easily across it.

DESIGNING THE BOARD:

1. Write the entire alphabet. You can arrange the letters across the top, across the bottom, in a circle, or in any other way you wish.

2. Write the numbers 0 through 9.

3. Write the words YES, NO, HELLO, and GOOD-BYE.

4. Decorate your board.

THE POINTER OR *PLANCHETTE*:

1. Use the small, clean jar or glass as your pointer.

2. Place it upside down on the board with your fingers on the bottom and ask the "spirits" your question. The glass will move, seemingly on its own, to spell out answers.

DISAPPEARING ACTS

Now you see them...now you don't.

THE LOST COLONY. In 1587, more than 100 men, women, and children traveled from England to Roanoke Island off North Carolina's coast and established the first English settlement in North America. Within three years, they disappeared. The colony's leader, Governor John White, had sailed back to England for supplies, and when he returned he found the fort empty of people and their belongings. The only clue to their whereabouts was the word CROATOAN carved into a post, with letters CRO carved into a nearby tree.

White and others searched for the lost colonists (including his granddaughter, America's first English baby, Virginia Dare)...but to no avail. Their disappearance remains a mystery. However, nearly 200 years later, British explorer John Lawson described a meeting with descendants of the Croatoan tribe. Many of them spoke English and were fair-haired. Could they have been descended from members of the lost colony?

THE VANISHING BATTALION. Three soldiers from a New Zealand field company witnessed the disappearance of an entire army battalion in World War I. It was 1915 and the soldiers watched as the Royal Norfolk Regiment marched up a hill at Suvla Bay, Turkey. A low-lying cloud covered the hill and the regiment marched straight into it. When the cloud lifted into the sky, the battalion of 267 men had disappeared. Their bodies were never found. There were no survivors. They did not turn up as prisoners of war. The entire battalion had simply vanished.

THE DISAPPEARANCE OF DAVID. It was a crisp fall day in September 1880 when David Lang headed off across the pasture to check on his horses. His children, George and Sarah, were playing in the yard of their Tennessee farm. Lang's wife, Emma, stood on the front porch, watching him go. David paused to wave at their friend Judge August Peck, who was trotting up the road in his horse and buggy. Seconds later, David Lang—in full view of his wife, his children, and the judge—disappeared in midstep. Emma screamed, thinking he had fallen into a hole. Everyone rushed to the spot where David had vanished, but there was no hole. They searched the area and found nothing. David was gone, never to be seen again. The Lang children later reported that a 15-foot circle of grass around the spot where their father had disappeared had wilted and turned yellow. Could that have had something to do with his disappearance? Many people believe it was hoax...but no one knows for sure.

TASTE THE MUSIC

*Believe it or not, some people can actually say,
"I like that song. It tastes like chocolate."*

Imagine every time you hear the phone ring...you taste spaghetti sauce. Or whenever you see the number three, it's blue. There are people who see colors when they hear music. And there are other people who not only see colors, but also taste sounds.

This strange ability has a name—*synesthesia*. It's from the Greek words for "together" and "perception," and means that the part of your brain that sees or hears mixes with the part of your brain that tastes or smells. As unusual as this sounds, one in 2,000 people has the condition.

One Swiss musician says that an F sharp makes her see violet and a C makes her see red. Minor chords makes her mouth taste sour or salty. Major chords make her mouth taste bitter or sweet. Some sounds have weird tastes like mown grass; others are as delicious as creamy milk.

THE HENGES

STONEHENGE is a circle of giant stones that stand on a plain in Great Britain. They align with the sun, moon, and stars and are estimated to be 5,000 years old. Who put them there? What are they for? Archaeologists believe it may have been an astronomical observatory, but no one really knows.

CARHENGE is a replica of Stonehenge created from vintage American automobiles. It juts up from the Nebraska plains on Highway 87 just outside the town of Alliance. Six local families at a reunion decided to build it in 1987. Why? Only they know for certain.

UFO CRASH SITE

Something *fell out of the sky near Roswell, New Mexico, on July 8, 1947. Was it a flying saucer? A test plane? Here's what happened that week:*

- **Friday:** Jim Ragsdale and Trudy Truelove claim to have seen a flying saucer crash into the desert and strange bodies—four to five feet tall—inside the wreckage.

- **Saturday:** Ragsdale and Truelove witness three army trucks hauling away all of the evidence from the crash site.

- **Sunday:** Local rancher William "Mack" Brazel hears about the crash and gives Major Jesse Marcel at Roswell Air Force Base some strange litter he found in the area. The scraps of metal cannot be cut or burned.

- **Monday:** Mortician Glenn Dennis gets an odd request from an Air Force officer for baby caskets. A nurse tells him she's just helped doctors autopsy strange little bodies.

- **Tuesday:** Base commander Colonel Blanchard issues a press statement: "We have in our possession a flying saucer."

- **Wednesday:** Blanchard's superior officer, General Roger Ramey, says no, the wreckage is just a weather balloon.

- **1970:** Retired Major Jesse Marcel comes forward and says that what he saw back in 1947 was no weather balloon! So, was it a flying saucer? What do *you* think?

UFO CENTRAL

One of the government's most secret locations.

Area 51—also known as Groom Lake—is part of Nellis Air Force Range in southern Nevada. It's a top-secret military base said to be a test-site for performing experiments on captured alien spacecraft. Want to see strange lights and hear weird sounds? Go there.

• Nevada State Highway 375, which runs south of Area 51, has been nicknamed "The Extraterrestrial Highway." Why? Many UFOs have been spotted along this lonely stretch of desert road.

• The stories about Area 51 were mostly just legend… until 1989 when respected scientist Bob Lazar came forward. Lazar told reporters that, in an attempt to unlock its secrets, he had actually worked on an alien spacecraft in 1988.

• Extra-terrestrials have short, gray bodies with almond-shaped eyes.

IT CAME FROM WAY OUT THERE

Falling stars and unidentified flying objects bring some pretty weird gifts.

STAR JELLY

Have you ever watched a falling star or a meteor rocket through the night sky? Most of them burn up in the atmosphere. But some actually hit the earth. Many people who have gone to the places where meteors hit report finding an odd, gooey substance that they call "star jelly." Unfortunately it evaporates pretty quicky, so it's hard to study. Some scientists think this jelly could be *nostoc*, an extremely adaptable type of blue-green algae that grows in clumps in the soil or floats on water. Others think the jelly might be an organism called "slime mold," which grows on the ground and can be

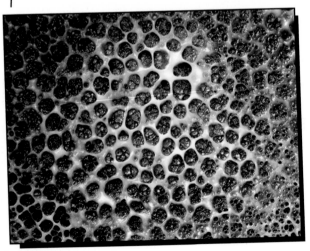

quite large. But whatever it is, no one has yet explained why this strange jelly appears where a meteor has fallen.

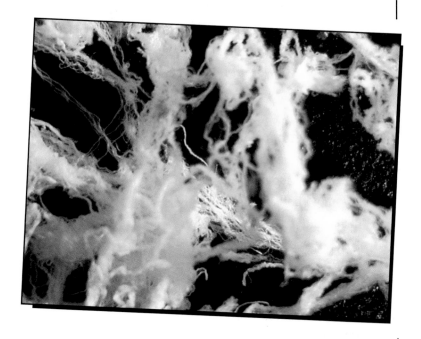

ANGEL HAIR

It is white and silky and looks like spiderwebs floating in the air. Dubbed "angel hair" by those who've seen it, these silky fibers generally appear during the sighting of a UFO. In October 1952, in the village of Oloron, France, high school superintendent Jean-Yves Prigent, his wife, and children, spied a cigar-shaped flying object hovering over their town surrounded by 30 smaller flying saucers. Ten days later 100 people saw the same thing in the town of Gaillac. Both times a substance like "angel hair" fell from the saucers. But when people tried to gather up the silky hair, it turned to jelly and evaporated into thin air.

THE GREEN CHILDREN OF WOOLPIT

Where did these legendary kids come from?

In 12th century England, during the reign of King Stephen, two very strange children were found alone near the town of Woolpit. Workers harvesting in a field heard the cries of a young boy and girl and found them huddled in an open pit, crying. But these were no ordinary children. They spoke a language that no one understood and they were dressed in clothes of an odd metallic material. Stranger still was the color of their skin—green!

The two green children were taken to the home of a man named Richard de Calne. It was difficult for de Calne to get them to eat or drink anything (all they would eat were beans, and only beans that were freshly cut from the beanstalks). The boy soon became ill and died, but the girl survived.

As she grew older and learned English, the green girl was finally able to tell her story, which was as remarkable as her appearance. She said that she and her brother had come from a place that had no sun. All the people there were green and they lived in a land of perpetual twilight. She said her home was across a river of light. When asked how they came to be in the pit, she said that they had heard bells, become mesmerized, and followed the sound of the bells into a cavern. When they emerged, they found themselves in the open pit and were "struck senseless" by the bright lights of our world.

The strange girl's skin faded as she grew up. She married a man from Norfolk, England, but never had any children. And the townspeople never knew if she had come from deep inside our planet or…another world. The green girl died a mystery.

RICE PORRIDGE

It's a breakfast cereal! No—it's a crystal ball.

Every year on February 26, a bowl of porridge is placed on the altar of the Chiriku Hachimangu Shrine in Japan. On March 15 the bowl is removed from the shrine and taken to the local fortune teller, who examines it and predicts what kind of harvest the village will have that year. This tradition has been going on for 1,200 years. In March 2005, the fortune teller spotted something unusual in the bowl of porridge: a crack cut through the shiny surface of the nearly month-old porridge. The fortune teller— Masahiro Higashi— saw the crack, and promptly warned people in the Kyushu area of an upcoming earthquake. Five days later Kyushu was shaken by a quake that measured a strong seven on the Richter scale and damaged more than 600 houses.

CROP CIRCLES

They appear overnight. What are they
and where do they come from?

On the night of July 16, 2002, mysterious lights appeared over the fields of Pewsey Downs in Wiltshire, England. The next morning an elaborate pattern shaped like a nautilus shell was carved into the field. Who made it... and why?

Sightings of crop circles go as far back as the 1970s when mysterious patterns that looked like giant pictures suddenly formed in farmers' fields. They have been seen in 29 countries and appear in wheat fields, corn fields, barley fields, rice paddies, and even in ice. They often appear near ancient sacred sites like Stonehenge in England and at crossing points of the earth's magnetic currents.

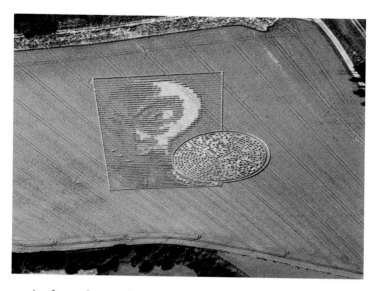

At first, the circles were simple geometric shapes that resembled the ancient Celtic cross. Then they became more elaborate pictograms that looked like ancient rock carvings. Since the 1990s the shapes have begun to mimic computer-generated geometric patterns containing elaborate mathematic equations.

IS IT A HOAX?

In 1991 two 70-year-old men named Doug Bower and Dave Chorley came forward to confess that in the 1970s they had made some of the crop circles using a piece of wood and rope. They even demonstrated on TV how they smashed down the corn to make the patterns. But "hoaxers" have been found to be responsible for only some of the crop circles. The others? Nobody's sure.

On July 8, 1996, a pilot flew over Stonehenge, England, and noted that all was normal below. Fifteen minutes later another pilot reported the formation of a 900-foot crop circle that contained 149 circles. It took surveyors 11 hours just to measure it!

THE REAL MCCOY

So, what makes a true crop circle? Usually the plants in the circles are bent, not broken. Quite often they are crisscrossed into as many as five layers. The circles have precise borders and contain very strong electromagnetic fields—sometimes strong enough to damage a digital camera or a computer. And many eyewitnesses have seen strange globes of light just before or during the formation of the circle.

If you want to actually see one for yourself, head for southern England in the summer. More than 90 percent of reported circles appear there.

ARE YOU A SLIDER?

Some people have strange powers over electrical appliances. You could be one of them.

When you walk under streetlights or drive by them, do they suddenly turn off or on? If so, you might be a SLIder, a person who appears to have an unusual effect on electrical lights and appliances. With SLIders, Street Lamp Interference (or SLI) doesn't happen once or twice, but all the time. SLIders say that when they are in an extreme emotional state, such as if they're mad, worried, or upset about something, streetlights often turn off.

SLIders also report that when they turn on lamps lightbulbs blow out, and they recount instances of TVs, electronic toys, radios, and CD players going off or on without being touched. SLIders insist that this weird "power" can't be controlled—it just happens.

Hillary Evans, author and paranormal investigator, has even established the Street Lamp Interference Data Exchange as a place for SLIders to share their experiences. So, if lights and TVs are going on and off when you walk by, you may want to get in touch with Evans. She wants to hear your story.

MORE AMAZING COINCIDENCES

R.S.V.P = R.I.P. In 1865 Robert Todd Lincoln was invited to attend a play with his parents. He arrived late to find that his father, Abraham Lincoln, had been assassinated. In 1881 President Garfield invited Robert to join him on a train trip. The president was killed at the station moments before Robert got on board. In 1901 President McKinley invited Robert to a public event. Seconds before Lincoln arrived, McKinley was shot. After that, Robert said he would accept no more presidential invitations, since three had invited him to their assassinations.

HELP! SAVE ME! Roger Lausier was four years old when he got caught in the surf near Salem, Massachusetts. A passing stranger named Alice Blaise rescued him. Nine years later, Lausier was swimming at the same beach when he heard a woman scream for help. Her husband was drowning. He quickly swam out and saved the man's life. Who was the woman? Alice Blaise.

SEA-MAIL. A Japanese sailor named Chunosake Matsuyama was shipwrecked in 1784. Before he and 44 shipmates died of starvation, Matsuyama carved a message on a piece of wood, sealed it in a bottle, and cast it into the sea. A century later the bottle washed up on the shore of a Japanese village—the very seaside village where Matsuyama was born.

THE SKY IS FALLING!

You expect rain, snow, sleet, and maybe even hailstones to come out of the sky...but you'd never expect this!

PENNIES FROM HEAVEN

One day in 1956, pennies rained down on children leaving school in Hanham, England. A year later thousands of 1,000 franc notes fell on the town of Bourges, France. No one ever reported any missing money. It just appeared from "way up there."

TAKE THAT!

Pinar del Río, Cuba, was pelted with mud, wood, glass, and broken pottery in four different rainfalls in 1968.

BLOOD AND GUTS

On August 27, 1968, flesh and blood rained onto an area of land between Cacapava and São José dos Campos, Brazil. The downpour lasted for almost seven minutes!

DUCK!

No one knows why more than a hundred ducks suddenly dropped out of the sky on St. Mary's City, Maryland, in January 1969. The ducks all had broken bones and injuries—but the injuries had happened to them *before* they fell.

382

FISH AND FROGS AND SNAKES, OH MY!

Reports of fish and reptiles falling from the sky are actually quite common. In 1877 thousands of live snakes dropped out of the sky on Memphis, Tennessee. Scientists speculated that the snakes were swept up by a hurricane, but could never determine where they came from, because there were no hurricanes nearby and no single location could have provided a home to that many snakes.

SPOON BENDING

Want to bend a spoon with your mind? We're not promising you'll be able to do it, but here's a good way to start: have a party!

Pyschokinesis, or PK, is all about mind over matter. People with pyschokinetic powers are said to be able to bend spoons without using any force. The famous spoon-bender Uri Geller claims that it's easy to learn how…and much easier if you are with a group of friends, having fun. Why? Because that's when your mind is in a state of "relaxed inattention"—the perfect time for spoon bending. Here's how:

1. INVITE LOTS OF FRIENDS

It's best to have friends who are curious, fun, and have a great sense of adventure.

2. HAVE LOTS OF SPOONS AVAILABLE

Each spoon bender should take time to find the right spoon. It helps to ask the spoon, "Do you want to bend for me?" Remember, not all spoons want to bend.

3. CLOSE YOUR EYES AND VISUALIZE

Imagine a ball of powerful, endless energy running down your arm and pouring into the spoon.

4. SHOUT LOUDLY AT THE SPOON

Take the spoon, hold it vertically in your hand and

shout, "Bend! Bend! Bend!" Don't skip this step. You've got to let the spoon know who's the boss.

5. LAUGH, GIGGLE, AND BE HAPPY

This is the most important step. When you're having lots of fun, your mind relaxes, making it possible for your spoon to bend.

6. BEND THE SPOON

Hold the spoon in one hand while rubbing it with the other hand. Don't use force—just use laughter. Really! If you worry about bending your spoon, it won't work.

7. BEND-MEISTER

Once you've mastered bending spoons, try bending two forks simultaneously with just your mind. Repeat all of the steps above, except this time you will hold two identical forks at the base, one in each hand. Imagine balls of energy running down your arms and into the forks. Don't forget to laugh.

NUM3ER MADNES5

Adding these random number-facts to your body of knowledge is as easy as one, two, three. (You can count on it!)

- Do you eat meat? If you do, in your lifetime you will devour 14 cows, 880 chickens, 23 pigs, 770 pounds of fish, 35 turkeys, and 12 sheep.

- A "jiffy" is an actual unit of time—it's $\frac{1}{100}$th of a second.

- In a normal eight-hour work day, a typist's fingers travel 12 miles.

- February 2, 2000 (2/2/2000) was the first date to contain only even numbers since August 8, 888 (8/08/888). That's 1,112 years earlier!

- November 19, 1999 (11/19/1999), was the last date containing only odd numbers. The next one will be January 1, 3111 (1/1/3111). That's 1,112 years later!

- Most people remember 20% of what they read, 30% of what they hear, 40% of what they see, 50% of what they say, and 60% of what they do.

- In movies or TV, when a telephone number is spoken or printed, it always begins with 555 because no home phone number begins with that prefix.

- If you watch television for one hour a night between the ages of six and 16, you will have spent eight waking months in front of the TV.

MORE...LOST AND FOUND

LOST: A rare orchid in New Zealand

FOUND: Under the tent of two botanists who had been searching for it for years—it was completely flattened!

LOST: A little girl in Dover, England, who drifted out to sea on a beach toy (an inflatable set of teeth) in 1994.

FOUND: Rescued by a man floating on an inflatable lobster.

LOST: A Christmas card that was mailed on December 23, 1903, to Elsa Johansson of Sweden.

FOUND: It finally arrived in 1985...82 years later.

SPOOKY SPOTS

Want to meet some real ghosts? Go to...

THE HAUNTED MANSION

One "D" ticket will get you on Disneyland's spookiest ride. Besides the ghosts created by Disney Imagineers, you might see a few real ones. Ghostly uninvited guests at the Haunted Mansion include a man in a tuxedo and an old man with a cane. But the saddest ghost of all is that of a young boy who sits near the exit, crying.

TOYS R US

"Ghosts R Us" might be a better name for this branch of the toy store chain in Sunnyvale, California, said to be haunted by a 19th-century rancher named Johnson. Dolls and toy trucks fly off shelves, books crash to the floor, and baby swings move on their own. Workers say they've felt him brush by or call them by name. Some won't use the ladies' room anymore because Johnson turns on the faucets.

SPANISH MILITARY HOSPITAL

This hospital-turned-museum in St. Augustine, Florida, was built on an ancient Indian burial ground, which may be why it has so many ghosts. Although there are strange growls, nasty smells, floating orbs, and sometimes dripping "ectoplasm" on the walls, director Diane Lane says the ghosts are really very nice—they open doors for her whenever she walks through the building.

EXTREME CASES

Don't laugh. It could happen to you!

HIC!

Charles Osborne could not stop hiccupping. This farmer started hic-ing in 1922, while weighing a pig just before slaughtering it. And for the next 68 years he hic-hic-hiccupped night and day. Sometimes he hiccupped so hard, his false teeth fell out. Over his lifetime he averaged 25 hiccups a minute. That's 430 million hiccups! When he finally stopped hiccupping, Osborne was 96 years old.

AH-CHOO!

Donna Griffiths was just an ordinary 12-year-old schoolgirl in Worcestershire, England, when the sneezing began. It was January 13, 1981—a day she will never forget. Griffiths estimates she sneezed over a million times in the first 365 days. Well-wishers from around the world sent her handkerchiefs and letters suggesting cures. At first she was sneezing at a rate of one sneeze a minute. By the third year, she had slowed to one every five minutes. And finally on September 16, 1983—978 days later—Griffiths stopped sneezing.

ROYAL WEIRDOS

Lifestyles of the rich and strange.

LIONEL WALTER ROTHSCHILD, 2nd Baron de Rothschild (1868–1937), drove a carriage drawn by four zebras. He also had a pet bear that liked to slap women on the butt, and he once hosted an important political dinner that included 12 impeccably dressed monkeys seated at the dinner table.

FRANCIS HENRY EGERTON, 8th Earl of Bridgewater (1756–1829), was known for giving extravagant dinner parties…for his dogs. The pups arrived dressed in the most fashionable clothing of the day (they even wore little shoes).

LUDWIG II of Bavaria (1845–1886) was an extremely shy man, a king who preferred fantasy to reality. He had imaginary dinners with favorite historical figures, and once brought his horse to dinner in the formal state dining room.

"Mad Ludwig" built fairy tale castles in the Bavarian Alps. Neuschwanstein, which means "new swan stone," is the most famous. The rooms were decorated with scenes from operas by his favorite composer, Richard Wagner. Ludwig made sure his dream house had hot and cold running water on every floor, flush toilets, and a central heating system. The castle was unfinished at the time of Ludwig's death in 1886.

KING FAROUK of Egypt (1920–1965) owned dozens of palaces, thousands of acres of land, and hundreds of cars. And he was a notorious pickpocket. The "Thief of Cairo" stole a pocket watch from Winston Churchill and a ceremonial sword right out of the casket of the Shah of Iran.

SNOOZE CLUES

According to Professor Chris Idzikowski of the Sleep Assessment and Advisory Service, your sleep position reveals your personality type. Which one are you?

1. FETAL: You are a little shy at first, but it doesn't take you long to warm up.

2. LOG: You are easygoing and trusting. You love being the center of activity.

3. YEARNER: You like to check your facts before you make up your mind. Once you've made a decision, you're committed to it.

4. SOLDIER: You are a quiet person, even a little reserved. You set high standards for yourself and others.

5. FREE-FALLER: You are ambitious and outgoing, sometimes even a little foolish. But ultimately, you'll never put yourself in an extreme situation.

6. STARFISH: You are a compassionate friend and good listener. You'd rather not be the center of attention.

Fetal   Log   Yearner   Soldier   Free-faller   Starfish

LAWN-CHAIR LARRY

This truck driver always wanted to fly, and at the age of 33 he finally did.

On July 2, 1982, Larry Walters tied 45 helium-filled weather balloons to an aluminum lawn chair in his backyard in San Pedro, California. Equipped with a bottle of soda, a camera, a CB radio, an altimeter, and a BB gun (for altitude control), Larry strapped on a parachute and climbed into his "aircraft"—the *Inspiration I.*

Before his friends could untie all the ropes, it broke loose. Seconds later Walters found himself floating at 16,000 feet. Startled pilots alerted air traffic control that a guy in a lawn chair was drifting into the approach to Long Beach airport.

The thin air was making Walters dizzy, so he popped several balloons with his BB gun and tried to land on a golf green. Instead, he got tangled up in some power lines. (He wasn't electrocuted, but he did cause a blackout over Long Beach.) Walters escaped with a $1,500 fine...and his life.

"Since I was 13, I've dreamed of going up into the sky in a weather balloon," Walters said later. "And by the grace of God, I fulfilled my dream. But I wouldn't do this again for anything!"

YOU'VE GOT MAIL

Can't find an envelope? Who cares?

According to government regulations, you can send almost anything through the United States Postal Service, as long as you follow these simple rules:

1. No dangerous chemicals, explosives, or glass.

2. No live animals.

3. Apply the correct postage.

Here are a few things that have actually been sent—unwrapped—but with the correct postage:

• **Money** (wrapped in clear plastic): a quarter, a $1 bill, and a $20 bill.

• **Clothing:** Brand-new tennis shoes; a sock tied to a set of keys.

• **Toys:** A football, a Lego postcard made out of actual Legos, and a toy monkey in a box. (When the box was shaken, the monkey screamed, "Let me out of here! Help! Let me out of here.")

•

Goofy stuff: A rose, a feather duster, a ski, a roll of toilet paper, and a message in a clear plastic bottle.

• **Food products:** A coconut, a wheel of smelly cheese, a wax peach.

PARTY ANIMALS

When you want to celebrate, what do you do?
Sing songs? Eat cake? When these guys celebrate
they go to strange (and scary) extremes.

BLOCO DE LAMA. Every year during Carnival in Brazil, these people dress up like cavemen, cover themselves in mud, and parade down the streets of the town of Paraty. The sulfurous mud is said to be good for the skin. But most just do it for the fun of it.

LA TOMATINA. The largest food fight on the planet takes place every year in Spain when 240,000 pounds of tomatoes are shipped into the small town of Bunol. More than 30,000 tourists make the journey to Bunol for the chance to hurl tomatoes at each other and be covered from head to toe in red slime.

FLUSHED AND FOUND

Top 20 most unusual items flushed down the toilet.

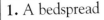

1. A bedspread

2. A possum

3. A pair of hiking boots

4. Fourteen pairs of men's extra-large briefs

5. False teeth

6. A wig

7. Rubber ducks

8. A rattlesnake

9. A seven-foot-long boa constrictor

10. Piranhas

11. TV remotes

12. An alarm clock

13. An 8-ball

14. Thirty golf balls

15. A bowling ball

16. A baseball bat

17. Twelve glass eyes

18. A bunch of $100 bills

19. A diamond

20. A Timex watch (still ticking…)

SHANNON SCAVOTTO

got the shock of his life when an African rock python reared up out of the toilet just as he was about to sit down. The six-foot-long snake has made the entire family think twice about using the toilet—especially in the dark.

BRITS AND THEIR "COMPS"

*Welcome to the quirky world
of British competition.*

BOG SNORKELING

Ever since 1985, the town of Llanwrtyd Wells, Wales, has hosted the Annual Peat Bog Competition. Competitors must swim two lengths of a 60-yard-long, muddy, reed-filled trench wearing snorkels and flippers. They can't use any conventional swim strokes, must not touch the bottom, and have to keep their faces in the muddy bog. The snorkeler with the fastest time wins.

CHEESE ROLLING

For hundreds of years, Cooper's Hill near Gloucester, England, has hosted an annual cheese roll. Cheese rolling may have started as an ancient fertility rite, but it has evolved into an all-out rollicking race down a very steep and extremely treacherous hill. At the start of the race an 8-pound, 3-inch-thick wheel of cheese is hurled down Coopers Hill. A moment later, the competitors run after the cheese. They never catch the cheese. By the time it reaches the bottom of the hill, the cheese is traveling 70 mph. Runners who are still on their feet when they reach the bottom of the hill (and very few make it that far) are tackled by rugby players to keep them from crashing into the fence at the end of the course. The first runner to cross the finish line gets to keep the cheese.

WORM CHARMING

In 1980 Tom Shufflebotham stunned the world by charming 511 worms out of the ground in 30 minutes at the first World Worm Charming Championships in Nantwich, Cheshire. Since then no one has been able to beat his record. How do you charm a worm? The most successful method is called "twanging"—inserting a four-pronged pitchfork in the ground and twanging it (vibrating it) until the worm crawls out. Under no circumstances can a competitor dig a worm out of the ground.

VAMPIRE BASICS

This simple guide will tell you everything you need to know about how to decide if your next door neighbor is a vampire.

THE TELLTALE SIGNS OF A VAMPIRE

• A vampire casts no reflection. It cannot be seen in a mirror or a photograph.

• A vampire is allergic to sunlight. It can only go out at night.

• Vampires cannot be heard over telephone lines.

• Vampires cannot or will not cross running water.

• Vampires are shape-shifters; they turn into bats, wolves, or wisps of smoke to travel.

• Vampires grow stronger as they get older.

HOW TO PROTECT YOURSELF

Garlic: Hang it around your neck. Rub it on your windows and doors. Garlic severely weakens a vampire.

Cross: Wear a cross around your neck. Crosses burn vampires.

Roses: Plant wild roses in your yard. Most vampires hate them.

Light: Keep your home well lit. A bright light will temporarily blind a vampire.

Hide the welcome mat: Whatever you do, never invite a vampire into your home. It cannot enter your house without your invitation.

STRANGE DEATHS

What a way to go!

SILENT BUT DEADLY

A man whose diet consisted of nothing but beans and cabbage was killed by his own farts. One night, while he was asleep, the noxious gas he "created" hovered over his bed and became so deadly that he never woke up. The three rescue workers called to the scene got sick, too—one even had to be taken to the hospital.

BLOWOUT

Children's entertainer Marlon Pistol was killed when a 20-foot-tall balloon elephant that he used in his act suddenly inflated in his tiny car as he drove along a California highway.

DRUMMED OUT OF TOWN

A Japanese man attempting to win the world record for nonstop drumming was stabbed to death by his neighbor, who just couldn't take one more beat.

HE PASTA WAY

When 150-mph winds hit chef Juan Ruiz's restaurant in Mexico City, he was stabbed through the heart by a flying strand of uncooked spaghetti.

THE LAST WORD
And that's final.

Here lies
the body of
Emily White

She signalled
left and then
turned right.

Here lies
Matthew Mudd,

Death did him
no hurt;

When he was alive he
was only Mudd,

Now he's
only dirt.

Once I
Wasn't.

Then I Was.

Now I ain't
Again.

Harry Edsel Smith
Born 1903
Died 1942

Looked up the
elevator shaft
To see
If the car was on
the way down.
It was.

403

POTTY ON, DUDE!

The queen of Pasadena, California's annual Doo Dah Parade is flush with pride as she sits serenely upon her throne and waves to crowds of adoring fans.

PHOTO CREDITS

Roy Rogers-Dale Evans Museum, Branson, Missouri (Trigger); **Page 144:** Getty Images (elephant); **Page 146:** Jay Newman (Porter the Wonder Dog); **Page 147:** Courtesy of the NORFANZ voyage partners-Australia's National Oceans Office and CSIRO and New Zealand's Ministry of Fisheries and NIWA. For more information, visit http://www.environment.gov.au/coasts/discovery/voyages/norfanz/index .html. Photo by Robin McPhee and Kerryn Parkinson; **Page 148:** iStockPhoto.com; **Page 151:** Courtesy of NOAA; **Page 152:** iStock-Photo.com; **Page 155:** Courtesy of NOAA; **Page 156:** © Phillip Colla, SeaPics.com; **Page 162:** BRI Photo Archives; **Page 163:** BigStockPhoto.com; **Page 166:** BRI photo archives; **Page 177:** BigStockPhoto.com; **Page 180:** BigStockPhoto.com; **Page 181:** BigStockPhoto.com; **Page 182:** AP Images; **Page 184:** © James D. Watt, SeaPics.com; **Page 188:** Getty Images; **Page 192:** iStockPhoto.com; **Page 195:** AP Images; **Page 197:** AP Images; **Page 201:** C. Ortlepp; **Page 205:** BigStockPhoto.com; **Page 211:** © Gordon M. Grant, *The New York Times*, Redux; **Page 214:** iStockPhoto.com; **Page 216:** Ansgar Walk, Wikimedia Commons; **Page 217:** NASA; **Page 218:** iStockPhoto.com; **Page 219:** Wikimedia Commons; **Page 221:** Wikimedia Commons; **Page 223:** AP Images; **Page 224:** Chris Gotschalk, Wikimedia Commons; **Page 225:** Zac Wolf, Wikimedia Commons (whale shark) / courtesy NOAA (megamouth); **Page 227:** iStockPhoto.com; **Page 228:** Wendy Rathey, Wikimedia Commons (leafy sea dragon) / Andy Murch, elasmodiver.com (tasseled wobbegong); **Page 229:** Massimo Boyer, www.kudalaut.eu (both photos); **Page 232:** NORFANZ (gulper eel) / Peter Herring, imagequestmarine.com (hairy angler): **Page 233:** Peter Herring, image-questmarine.com; **Page 234:** NASA; **Page 242:** BigStockPhoto.com (sawfish) / iStockPhoto.com (great white shark) / Wikimedia Commons (narwhals); **Page 246:** BigStockPhoto.com; **Page 251:** iStockPhoto.com; **Page 252:** Wikimedia Commons; **Page 254:** © 2004 Ingrid Visser, SeaPics.com; **Page 257:** NASA; **Page 258:** BRI Photo Archives; **Page 260:** Wikimedia Commons; **Pages 261 & 262:** BigStockPhoto.com; **Page 264:** Chris 73, Wikimedia Commons; **Page 265:** Islands in the Stream Expedition 2002, NOAA Office of Ocean Exploration (puffer fish) / Filip Stachowiak, Wikimedia Commons (surstromming can); **Page 269:** Wikimedia Commons; **Page 274:** AquaOne Technologies, LLC, www.aquaone.com; **Page 276:** Jay Newman (Porter the Wonder Dog); **Page 277:** Splash News (Cabbage Patch Kid); **Page 278:** Jay Newman (sneaker); **Page 279:** AP Images (shoe tree); **Page 283:** Jay Newman (Ned's Head)/Jay Newman (Furbies); **Page 286:** Gordon Cates, Herpetologist, 954-646-5262, Photo Courtesy of www.teddgreenwald.com (Gordon Cates); **Page 287:**

Reuters (Scorpion Queen); **Page 291:** Graham Barker (navel fluff); **Page 293:** Getty Images (Jesus Manuel Aceves); **Page 295:** Reuters (Greg Smith); **Page 296:** Jolyn Morehead, Ambiance Photographer (Tyson and Treyson Neff); **Page 298:** iStockPhotos.com (waitress); **Page 302:** Stock.Xchng (King Tut); **Page 304:** Library of Congress (mummy); **Page 305:** Caitlin Maddigan (illustration: Preparing the Body); **Page 310:** Marion Cemetery Association (Merchant Ball Tombstone); **Page 313:** Karen Underwood, www.cotswoldedge.org (Ram Inn Fireplace); **Page 314:** Caitlin Maddigan (illustration: Ta Moko); **Page 315:** Library of Congress (Maori king); **Page 318:** Jay Newman (tea cup and tea leaves); **Page 320:** iStock.com (chimpanzee); **Page 323:** W. Stoneham, www.stonehamstudios.com (painting, *The Hands Resist Him*); **Page 326:** Jay Newman (cane); **Page 328:** Getty Images (creative coffins); **Page 337:** Stock.Xchng (toilet); **Page 338:** Liza Burdukova (Troye Wallett, Wolfberg Cracks, Cederberg, South Africa); **Page 339:** The Egremont Crab Fair & Sports, www.egremontcrabfair.org.uk (Gurning Champion, Kath Taylor); **Page 343:** BRI Photo Archives (Joseph Merrick); **Page 346:** iStockPhotos.com (mold) / American Academy of Allergy, Asthma and Immunology (dust mite) / iStockPhotos.com (fly); **Page 347:** iStockPhotos.com (closeup fly) / iStockPhotos.com (bacteria) / iStockPhotos.com (tick) / iStockPhotos.com (Spider); **Page 348:** BRI Photo Archives (winning ticket); **Page 351:** Jay Newman (Uncle John's Groucho Gathering); **Page 354:** Getty Images (Albert Einstein); **Page 355:** Library of Congress (Galileo); **Page 359:** Getty Images (Erik Sprague); **Page 363:** Stock.Xchng, Sam Rusling photographer (rat) / Stock.Xchng (scorpion) / Stock.Xchng (Roach); **Page 364:** © Copyright, Lewis Barrett Lehrman for the Haunted Studio, www.HauntedStudio.com, www.PortalsToTheBeyond.com (13 Spooks, Maybe More Ouija Board); **Page 365:** © Kipling West 2006 (Black Jack with the Hackle Back Ouija Board); **Page 369:** Stock.Xchng (Stonehenge)/The Stock Exchange (Car Henge); **Page 371:** Stock.Xchng; Can Berkol, photographer (alien); **Page 372:** iStockphotos.com (slime mold); **Page 373:** Frontier Analysis, Ltd. (angel hair); **Page 376:** iStockphotos.com (monk); **Page 377:** Lucy Pringle, www.lucypringle.co.uk (Nautilus crop circle) **Page 378:** Lucy Pringle, www.lucypringle.co.uk (Sparsholt Face crop circle); **Page 379:** Lucy Pringle, www.lucypringle.co.uk (Fractals crop circle); **Page 385:** Jay Newman (bent spoons); **Page 390:** © The Natural History Museum, London (Sir Lionel Walter Rothschild); **Page 391:** Library of Congress (Castle Neuschwanstein); **Page 393:** AP Images (Larry Walters); **Page 394:** Jay Newman (coconut); **Page 395:** Reuters Pictures (Bloco de Lama mud man); **Page 396:** Getty Images (La Tomatina); **Page 398:** Copyright © Bog Snorkelling Australia, http://bogsnorkelling.com (Bog Snorkeling competitor); **Page 404:** AP Images (Giant Toilet Float, Doo Dah Parade).

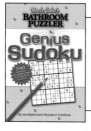
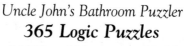

Want More Great Reading?
Look for All of These
Bathroom Readers
For Kids Only!

Uncle John's
Bathroom Reader
FOR KIDS ONLY!
©2002 • $12.95
288 pages, illustrated

Uncle John's
ELECTRIFYING
Bathroom Reader
For Kids Only!
©2003 • $12.95
288 pages, illustrated

Uncle John's
TOP SECRET!
Bathroom Reader
For Kids Only!
©2004 • $12.95
288 pages, illustrated

Uncle John's
BOOK OF FUN
©2004 • $12.95
288 pages, illustrated

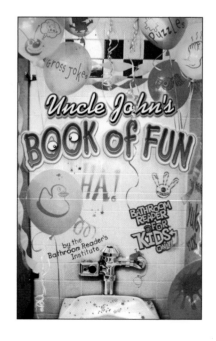

THE LAST PAGE

FELLOW BATHROOM READERS
Bathroom reading should never be taken loosely, so Sit Down and Be Counted! Join the Bathroom Readers' Institute. Just go to *www.bathroomreader.com* to sign up. It's free! Or send a self-addressed, stamped envelope and your e-mail address to: Bathroom Readers' Institute, P.O. Box 1117, Ashland, Oregon 97520. You'll receive our BRI newsletter (sent out via e-mail), discounts when ordering directly through the BRI, and you'll earn a permanent spot on the BRI honor roll!

UNCLE JOHN'S NEXT
BATHROOM READER FOR KIDS ONLY
IS ALREADY IN THE WORKS!

Is there a subject you'd like to read about in our next *Uncle John's Bathroom Reader* for kids? Write to us at *www.bathroomreader.com* and let us know. We aim to please.

Well, we're out of space, and when you've got to go, you've got to go. Hope to hear from you soon. Meanwhile, remember…

Go with the Flow!